Southern Living.

COMFORT FOOD IN A BOWL

Southern Living®

COMFORT FOOD IN A BOWL

Oxmoor House®

contents

Mexican Tomato
Soup, page 27

chicken
and
seafood
soups

southern italian chicken soup

makes 8 servings · hands-on time 45 min. · total time 50 min.

Fresh Parmigiano-Reggiano has a rich, sharp flavor that you can't get from the pre-grated varieties. It is a little more expensive, but less goes a long way.

1 large onion, diced
1 celery rib, thinly sliced
2 carrots, chopped
1 garlic clove, minced
3 Tbsp. olive oil, divided
6 cups chicken broth
1 (15.5-oz.) can diced tomatoes
1 tsp. dried Italian seasoning
¼ tsp. dried crushed red pepper

4 (6- to 8-oz.) skinned and boned chicken breasts
½ tsp. table salt
½ tsp. black pepper
2 cups sliced fresh okra
1 (15.5-oz.) can black-eyed peas, drained and rinsed
1 (9-oz.) package refrigerated cheese-filled tortellini
Freshly shaved Parmigiano-Reggiano cheese

1. Sauté first 4 ingredients in 2 Tbsp. hot oil in a large Dutch oven over medium-high heat 3 to 5 minutes or until tender. Stir in broth and next 3 ingredients; bring to a boil, stirring occasionally. Reduce heat to medium, and simmer, stirring occasionally, 10 minutes.

2. Meanwhile, sprinkle chicken with salt and black pepper. Cook in remaining 1 Tbsp. hot oil in a large nonstick skillet over medium-high heat 5 minutes on each side or until lightly browned. Cool slightly (about 5 minutes); cut into 1-inch pieces.

3. Add okra, black-eyed peas, and chicken to Dutch oven. Simmer, stirring occasionally, 10 minutes or until okra is tender. Add tortellini, and cook, stirring occasionally, 3 minutes or until tortellini is done. Serve with Parmigiano-Reggiano.

lemon-chicken soup

makes 5½ qt. · hands-on time 30 min. · total time 2 hours, 15 min.

6   skin-on, bone-in chicken
    breasts
2   large onions, chopped
5   celery ribs, chopped
2   garlic cloves, minced
1   tsp. olive oil
1   (1-lb.) package carrots,
    diagonally sliced

4   tsp. lemon zest
2   bay leaves
2   tsp. table salt
½   cup loosely packed fresh
    flat-leaf parsley leaves
Toppings: cooked barley,
    cooked green beans,
    lemon slices

souper tip

Rub the lemon against a
Microplane zester, only
removing the yellow
skin and not the white
pith, which tends to
have a bitter flavor.

1. Bring chicken and water to cover to a boil in a Dutch oven over medium-high heat; reduce heat to low, and simmer 1 hour.

2. Remove chicken, reserving liquid, and let cool 15 minutes. Shred chicken.

3. Pour reserved cooking liquid through a fine wire-mesh strainer into a bowl, discarding solids; wipe Dutch oven clean. Add water to cooking liquid to equal 10 cups.

4. Sauté onion, celery, and garlic in hot oil in Dutch oven over medium-high heat 5 to 6 minutes or until tender. Add shredded chicken, cooking liquid, carrots, and next 3 ingredients. Cover, reduce heat to medium, and cook 20 minutes or until carrots are tender. Remove and discard bay leaves. Add parsley. Serve with desired toppings.

Note: Freeze any leftovers in small containers for lunches and when someone has a case of the sniffles.

matzo ball soup

makes about 3½ qt. · hands-on time 30 min. · total time 4 hours

....

1   **(1-oz.) package fresh dill**
1   **bunch fresh parsley**
Kitchen string
3   **skin-on, bone-in chicken**
    breasts (about 3 lb.)
1   **medium onion, quartered**
4   **medium carrots, thinly**
    sliced
3   **parsnips, thinly sliced**
3   **celery ribs**

2   **Tbsp. vegetable oil**
4   **large eggs, lightly beaten**
1   **cup matzo meal**
1¾ **tsp. kosher salt**
1½ **to 2 Tbsp. fresh lemon**
    juice
2½ **tsp. kosher salt**
½ **tsp. ground white pepper**
Fresh dill sprigs

1. Tie half of dill and half of parsley in a bunch with kitchen string. Chop remaining dill and parsley to equal 2 tsp. each.

2. Bring chicken, next 4 ingredients, dill-parsley bunch, and 3½ qt. water to a boil in a large Dutch oven over medium-high heat; skim any foam with a slotted spoon. Cover, reduce heat to medium-low, and simmer 2½ to 3 hours or until chicken is tender and falls off the bone.

3. Meanwhile, whisk together oil, eggs, and ¼ cup water. Add matzo meal and 1¾ tsp. kosher salt; whisk until well blended. Cover and chill 30 minutes.

4. Remove soup from heat. Skim fat from surface of broth. Remove chicken and celery. Pour broth through a fine wire-mesh strainer into a large bowl. Return broth, carrots, and parsnips to Dutch oven, discarding onion and herb bunch. Let chicken, celery, and broth mixture cool 30 minutes.

5. Meanwhile, shape matzo batter into 18 (1-inch) balls (about 1 Tbsp. each), using wet hands. Bring 2½ qt. water to a boil in a large saucepan over medium-high heat. Drop matzo balls into boiling water; return to a boil. Cover, reduce heat to medium-low; simmer 30 minutes. Remove matzo balls from water with a slotted spoon.

6. Squeeze juice from cooled celery ribs into broth. Discard celery ribs. Skin and bone chicken; shred chicken. Add matzo balls, shredded chicken, lemon juice, 2½ tsp. kosher salt, and pepper to broth. Bring to a boil over medium-high heat. Reduce heat to medium-low; simmer 8 minutes. Stir in reserved dill and parsley; cook 2 minutes.

chicken, mushroom, and wild rice soup

makes 14 cups · hands-on time 40 min. · total time 40 min.

souper tip

Cooking the rice mix in the chicken broth infuses it with a lot of additional flavor. When preparing rice for a side dish, try cooking it in chicken, vegetable, or beef broth instead of water.

2 (6-oz.) packages long-grain and wild rice mix
10 cups chicken broth, divided
3 Tbsp. butter
1 cup sliced fresh mushrooms
1 cup chopped onion
1 cup chopped celery
¼ cup butter
½ cup all-purpose flour
½ cup half-and-half
2 Tbsp. dry white wine
2 cups cooked shredded chicken breasts
Garnishes: fresh parsley leaves, freshly cracked pepper

1. Bring rice, 4 cups chicken broth, and 1 seasoning packet from rice mix to a boil in a saucepan over medium-high heat. Cover, reduce heat to low, and simmer 20 minutes or until liquid is absorbed and rice is tender. (Reserve remaining seasoning packet for another use.)

2. Meanwhile, melt 3 Tbsp. butter in a large skillet over medium heat; add mushrooms, onion, and celery, and cook, stirring often, 10 to 12 minutes or until tender.

3. Melt ¼ cup butter in a Dutch oven over medium heat; whisk in flour, and cook, whisking constantly, 1 minute, or until thickened and bubbly. Gradually whisk in remaining 6 cups broth, and cook, stirring often, 8 to 10 minutes or until slightly thickened. Whisk in half-and-half and wine. Stir in mushroom mixture, chicken, and rice. Cook, stirring occasionally, 5 to 10 minutes or until thoroughly heated. (Do not boil.)

break down a rotisserie chicken

Consider these tips when preparing and using a rotisserie chicken

It's easiest to cut up a rotisserie chicken when it's warm. Either cut it up as soon as you come home from the grocery store, or warm the chicken for 15 minutes in a 350° oven.

- Cut all twine from the chicken, including the pieces that tie the legs together.
- If at all possible, use a boning knife to break down the chicken. The thin, narrow blade makes it easy to cut into tight spaces accurately and cleanly.
- The average chicken yields about 3 cups chopped or shredded meat.

Here's how to prepare the chicken exactly how you need it for each recipe:

Shredded: Using 2 forks, pull the chicken in opposite directions to shred it.

- Perfect for saucy dishes like pastas and casseroles, on sandwiches topped with dressings and sauces (like barbecue), or as a pizza topping
- Great way to use every bit of rotisserie chicken

Chopped: Cut chicken breast into bite-size cubes

- The chicken holds its shape in the finished dish
- Use it in chicken salad or stuffed potatoes

Sliced: Cut chicken breast into ¼-inch slices

- Makes a beautiful presentation when topping a dish like pasta or to make a salad a main dish

Start by removing the legs. Place the chicken on a cutting board, breast side up. Pull the leg and thigh away from the chicken, and cut through the connective joint.

To separate the thigh from the drumstick, pull the drumstick away from the thigh, and cut through the connective joint.

Make a deep horizontal cut above each wing.

Make a deep vertical cut along both sides of the breastbone.

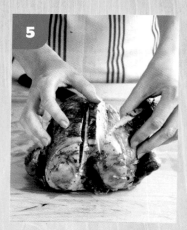

Remove the breast meat to chop or shred, or carve it in slices, starting from the outer edges and working inward.

Remove the wings from the chicken by pulling the wing away from the chicken body, and cutting through the wing joint.

pozole

makes 6 to 8 servings · hands-on time 1 hour · total time 4 hours, 5 min.

1 (3-lb.) whole chicken
1 lb. tomatillos, husks removed
2 jalapeño peppers, stemmed
1 medium-size yellow onion, chopped
6 garlic cloves
1 (29-oz.) can Mexican-style or other canned hominy, drained
1 (28-oz.) can crushed tomatoes
2 Tbsp. dried Mexican oregano
4 dried bay leaves
2 dried cascabel chiles, stemmed
½ cup hot water
2 tsp. table salt
Lime wedges

souper tip

You can top this soup with a variety of fresh herbs and vegetables to add color and crunch. Try fresh cilantro, sliced jalapeños, charred corn kernels, sliced radishes, or shredded cabbage.

1. Bring 6 qt. water to a boil over high heat in an 8-qt. stockpot. Remove neck and giblets from chicken. Add chicken, neck, and giblets to boiling water. Return to a boil; cook 15 minutes. Cover, remove from heat, and let stand 20 minutes. Transfer chicken to a plate, reserving broth in stockpot; discard neck and giblets. Cover and chill chicken until cool enough to handle.

2. Meanwhile, combine tomatillos, next 3 ingredients, and 2½ cups reserved broth in a medium saucepan. Bring to a rolling boil over medium-high heat, and cook, stirring occasionally, 20 minutes or until garlic is very soft.

3. Skin, bone, and shred chicken, reserving bones, skin, and any juices. Cover and chill chicken until ready to use. Return skin, bones, and juices to broth in stockpot. Bring to a rolling boil over medium-high heat; cook 30 to 45 minutes or until the bones begin to separate. Pour mixture through a fine wire-mesh strainer into a large bowl, discarding solids. Return to pot. Skim fat from broth. Bring broth to a simmer over medium-high heat.

4. Process tomatillo mixture in a blender or food processor until smooth. Stir into broth. Stir in hominy and next 3 ingredients; bring to boil. Reduce heat to medium-low; cover and simmer, stirring occasionally, 1 hour. Remove and discard bay leaves.

5. Meanwhile, soak chiles in ½ cup hot water in a small bowl for 30 minutes. Drain, reserving soaking liquid. Process chiles and 2 to 3 Tbsp. soaking liquid in a blender or food processor until smooth. Stir 2 tsp. salt and pepper to taste into broth. Pour chile mixture through a fine wire-mesh strainer into broth, discarding solids. Stir in shredded chicken, and simmer 15 minutes. Serve with lime wedges.

chicken tortilla soup

makes 10 cups · hands-on time 10 min. · total time 7 hours, 10 min.

Chicken thighs work beautifully in this recipe. And cooking them nice and slowly yields perfectly tender meat.

1¾ lb. skinned and boned chicken thighs
1 (12-oz.) bag frozen whole kernel yellow corn, thawed
1 large onion, chopped
2 garlic cloves, pressed
2 (14-oz.) cans reduced-sodium fat-free chicken broth
1 (14-oz.) can tomato puree
1 (10-oz.) can diced tomatoes and green chiles
1 tsp. smoked paprika
2 tsp. ground cumin
1 tsp. chili powder
1 bay leaf
4 (5½-inch) corn tortillas
Lime wedges
Toppings: fresh cilantro leaves, shredded Cheddar cheese, sliced jalapeños, and avocados

1. Combine first 11 ingredients in a 4-qt. slow cooker.

2. Cover and cook on HIGH 7 to 8 hours. Discard bay leaf, and shred chicken.

3. Preheat oven to 375°. Cut tortillas into ¼-inch-wide strips, and place on a baking sheet.

4. Bake at 375° for 5 minutes. Stir and bake 5 more minutes or until crisp. Add salt to taste. Serve soup with tortilla strips, lime wedges, and toppings.

quick chicken noodle bowls

makes 6 servings · hands-on time 20 min. · total time 45 min.

souper tip

Bringing the broth back to a boil before serving ensures the snap peas cook to a crisp-tender texture.

6 cups chicken broth
4 skinned and boned chicken thighs (about 1 lb.)
⅓ cup sliced fresh ginger
2 garlic cloves, sliced
⅛ tsp. Chinese five spice
1 (9.5-oz.) package soba noodles or 8 oz. angel hair pasta

1 Tbsp. soy sauce
Toppings: halved sugar snap peas, fresh cilantro and mint leaves, thinly sliced green onions, thinly sliced red chile peppers
2 to 3 Tbsp. fresh lime juice

1. Bring first 5 ingredients to a boil in a 3-qt. saucepan over medium heat. Cover, reduce heat to low, and simmer 6 to 8 minutes or until chicken is done. Remove chicken, garlic, and ginger with a slotted spoon, reserving broth in saucepan. Discard garlic and ginger. Let chicken cool slightly (10 to 15 minutes); shred chicken.

2. Return broth to a boil over medium heat. Add noodles and soy sauce; cook, stirring to separate noodles, 4 to 5 minutes or until just softened. Remove noodles from broth using tongs, and divide among 6 bowls. Place chicken and desired toppings on noodles. Return broth to a boil over medium heat; remove from heat, and stir in lime juice. Divide broth among bowls.

chicken 'n' white bean soup

makes 12 cups · hands-on time 20 min. · total time 1 hour, 5 min.

Great Northern beans have a wonderful creamy texture that's an ideal textural contrast in this rustic soup. Serve with crusty bread on the side.

1	Tbsp. butter
4	skinned and boned chicken breast halves, chopped
1	large onion, chopped
3	carrots, chopped
2	garlic cloves, minced
2	(14-oz.) cans low-sodium chicken broth
1	Tbsp. chicken bouillon granules
1	tsp. ground cumin
¼	tsp. ground red pepper
3	(16-oz.) cans great Northern beans, rinsed, drained, and divided
1	(4.5-oz.) can chopped green chiles
2	Tbsp. all-purpose flour
½	cup milk
¼	cup chopped fresh cilantro
Toppings:	shredded Cheddar cheese, sour cream, sliced green onions, cooked and crumbled bacon

1. Melt butter in a large Dutch oven over medium-high heat; add chicken and next 3 ingredients, and sauté 10 minutes. Stir in broth and next 3 ingredients.

2. Bring to a boil; reduce heat, and simmer, stirring occasionally, 20 minutes. Stir in 2 cans of beans and chiles.

3. Mash remaining can of beans in a small bowl. Whisk together flour and milk, and stir into beans. Gradually add bean mixture to soup mixture, stirring constantly. Cook 10 minutes or until thickened. Remove from heat, and stir in cilantro. Serve with desired toppings.

alphabet chicken soup

makes about 10 cups · hands-on time 10 min. · total time 39 min.

- 1 medium onion, chopped
- 2 carrots, chopped
- 2 celery ribs, chopped
- 1 Tbsp. vegetable oil
- 2 garlic cloves, minced
- 2 (32-oz.) containers chicken broth (8 cups)
- 2 cups Seasoned Shredded Chicken
- ¼ tsp. dried thyme
- ½ cup alphabet-shaped pasta, uncooked

souper tip

If you want to use homemade broth but don't quite have 8 cups, use commercial broth to make up the difference. Any small pasta will work in this recipe.

1. Sauté first 3 ingredients in hot oil in a Dutch oven over medium-high heat 5 minutes; add garlic, and sauté 1 minute. Stir in broth, chicken, thyme, and salt and pepper to taste. Bring to a boil; reduce heat, and simmer, stirring occasionally, 15 minutes. Stir in pasta, and cook 8 more minutes.

seasoned shredded chicken

makes about 6 cups · hands-on time 5 min. · total time 30 min.

- 6 skinned, bone-in chicken breasts
- 6 chicken bouillon cubes

1. Bring chicken, water to cover, and bouillon cubes to a boil over medium-high heat in a large saucepan. Reduce heat, and simmer 20 to 25 minutes or until chicken is done.

2. Remove chicken from broth, reserving broth, and cool slightly; pull meat from bones, and shred with a fork, discarding bones. Sprinkle with salt and seasoned pepper to taste. Place in quart-size zip-top plastic freezer bags, and freeze up to 1 month. Thaw in refrigerator overnight.

3. Strain reserved broth into an airtight container, and store in refrigerator for up to 1 week and in the freezer up to 3 months.

mexican tomato soup

makes 4 to 6 servings · hands-on time 1 hour, 5 min. · total time 1 hour, 40 min.

6 (6-inch) corn tortillas
2 Tbsp. canola oil, divided
2 medium tomatoes, cored and halved
1 onion, chopped
2 garlic cloves
1 (32-oz.) container reduced-sodium fat-free chicken broth
2 cups low-sodium tomato juice
1 bay leaf
¼ tsp. ground cumin
¼ tsp. ground coriander
¼ tsp. ground red pepper
1½ lb. skinned and boned chicken breasts, cut into ½-inch-wide strips
4 green onions (white part only), thinly sliced
½ cup fresh lime juice
¼ cup chopped fresh cilantro
½ cup crumbled queso fresco (fresh Mexican cheese)
1 medium avocado, chopped

souper tip

Charring the tomatoes adds a wonderfully smoky dimension to this zesty soup.

1. Preheat oven to 400°. Brush 1 side of tortillas with 1 Tbsp. oil; cut tortillas in half. Stack tortilla halves; cut crosswise into ¼-inch-wide strips. Arrange in a single layer on a lightly greased baking sheet. Season with salt and pepper. Bake at 400° for 15 minutes or until golden, stirring halfway through. Cool.

2. Meanwhile, heat a nonstick skillet over high heat 2 minutes. Add tomato halves, and cook, turning occasionally, 10 minutes or until charred on all sides. (Tomatoes may stick.) Transfer to a food processor.

3. Sauté onion in remaining 1 Tbsp. hot oil in skillet over medium heat 3 to 5 minutes or until tender. Add garlic; sauté 2 minutes or until fragrant. Transfer onion mixture to food processor with tomatoes; process until smooth.

4. Cook tomato mixture in a Dutch oven over medium-high heat, stirring occasionally, 5 minutes or until thickened. Stir in broth and tomato juice. Add bay leaf and next 3 ingredients; bring to a boil. Reduce heat to medium-low, and simmer, partially covered and stirring occasionally, 20 minutes.

5. Add chicken; simmer, stirring occasionally, 5 to 7 minutes or until chicken is done. Discard bay leaf. Stir in green onions and next 2 ingredients. Season with salt and pepper. Divide queso fresco among 4 to 6 soup bowls; top with tortilla strips. Ladle soup into bowls. Top with avocado.

lemon, orzo, and meatball soup

makes about 3 qt. · hands-on time 30 min. · total time 55 min.

1 lb. ground chicken
1 large egg, lightly beaten
¼ cup fine, dry breadcrumbs
1 tsp. kosher salt
4 tsp. loosely packed lemon zest, divided
1 tsp. dried crushed rosemary, divided
3 Tbsp. olive oil, divided
1 medium-size sweet onion, chopped
3 carrots, thinly sliced
2 garlic cloves, minced
2 (32-oz.) containers chicken broth
5 to 6 Tbsp. lemon juice
¾ cup orzo pasta
¼ cup freshly grated Parmesan cheese
½ cup fresh flat-leaf parsley leaves

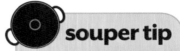

souper tip

To keep the chicken mixture from sticking to your hands when shaping the meatballs, coat your hands with a little cooking spray.

1. Combine first 4 ingredients, 2 tsp. lemon zest, and ½ tsp. rosemary in a medium bowl. Shape into 30 (1-inch) meatballs (about 1 level teaspoonful each).

2. Sauté meatballs, in 2 batches, in 1 Tbsp. hot oil per batch in a Dutch oven over medium heat 3 to 4 minutes or until browned. Remove using a slotted spoon.

3. Sauté onion and next 2 ingredients in remaining 1 Tbsp. hot oil in Dutch oven over medium-high heat 3 to 5 minutes or until tender. Stir in broth, lemon juice, and remaining 2 tsp. zest and ½ tsp. rosemary. Bring to a boil, stirring occasionally. Add orzo. Reduce heat to medium; simmer, stirring occasionally, 7 to 9 minutes or until pasta is almost tender.

4. Stir in meatballs; simmer, stirring occasionally, 5 to 7 minutes or until meatballs are thoroughly cooked. Add salt and pepper to taste. Top with cheese and parsley.

fiesta turkey soup with green chile biscuits

makes 8 servings · hands-on time 15 min. · total time 45 min.

1 medium onion, diced
1 tsp. vegetable oil
1 garlic clove, minced
3 cups chopped cooked turkey or chicken
1 (15-oz.) can chili beans
3½ cups chicken or turkey broth
1 (11-oz.) can whole kernel corn with red and green peppers, drained
1 (10-oz.) can diced tomatoes and green chiles
½ tsp. chili powder
½ tsp. ground cumin
⅛ tsp. table salt
⅛ tsp. black pepper
Toppings: sour cream, shredded Mexican four-cheese blend
Green Chile Biscuits (page 200)

1. Sauté onion in hot oil in a large Dutch oven over medium heat 7 minutes or until tender. Add garlic, and sauté 1 minute. Stir in turkey and next 8 ingredients. Bring to a boil, stirring occasionally; reduce heat, and simmer 15 minutes. Serve with desired toppings and Green Chile Biscuits.

tortilla turkey soup

makes 8 cups · hands-on time 30 min. · total time 40 min.

10 (6-inch) fajita-size corn
   tortillas, cut into ½-inch-
   wide strips
Vegetable cooking spray
1 small onion, chopped
2 garlic cloves, chopped
1 small jalapeño pepper,
   seeded and minced
1 Tbsp. olive oil
1 (32-oz.) container chicken
   broth

1 (10-oz.) can medium
   enchilada sauce
2 cups chopped cooked
   turkey
1 tsp. ground cumin
Toppings: chopped avocado,
   shredded sharp Cheddar
   cheese, chopped fresh
   cilantro, chopped
   tomatoes

souper tip

When buying fresh cilantro, choose a bunch that has bright, green leaves that show no signs of yellowing or wilting. To store, place the stems (with roots intact, if attached) in a glass of water, cover the top loosely with a plastic bag, and refrigerate. Snip off the leaves as you need them, and re-cover. Change the water every two to three days to keep the cilantro fresh longer. Do not wash the herb until you are ready to use it, as excess moisture ruins the leaves during storage.

1. Preheat oven to 450°. Place half of tortilla strips in a single layer on a baking sheet. Coat strips with cooking spray; bake 10 minutes or until browned and crisp, stirring once.

2. Sauté onion and next 2 ingredients in hot oil in a Dutch oven over medium-high heat 5 to 6 minutes or until browned.

3. Add chicken broth and remaining unbaked tortilla strips to onion mixture. Cook broth mixture over medium heat 3 to 5 minutes or until tortilla strips soften and broth mixture thickens slightly.

4. Stir in enchilada sauce and next 2 ingredients, and cook 6 to 8 minutes or until mixture is thoroughly heated. (Do not boil.) Serve with baked tortilla strips and desired toppings.

sweet corn soup with crab

makes 10½ cups · hands-on time 25 min. · total time 1 hour, 5 min.

souper tip

When fresh corn is in season, you can use the cobs to make a homemade stock. Place the cobs in water to barely cover in a large Dutch oven, and bring to a low boil. Reduce the heat, and simmer for about an hour. Discard the cobs. Store the stock in an airtight container in the refrigerator for up to three days. Use it as you would any stock: to deglaze a pan for a flavorful sauce, as the base for a brothy soup, or to add a bit of flavor to a sauté of fresh vegetables.

⅓ cup diced salt pork
2 Tbsp. butter
¼ cup white cornmeal
2 celery ribs, diced
1 medium onion, diced
1 red bell pepper, diced
1 jalapeño pepper, diced
3 cups fresh sweet corn kernels (about 6 ears)

4¾ cups chicken broth
2 corncobs
1 lb. fresh lump crabmeat, drained
1 cup whipping cream
¼ cup chopped fresh cilantro
½ tsp. table salt
¼ tsp. ground white pepper
Garnish: fresh cilantro leaves

1. Brown salt pork in a Dutch oven over medium heat; remove pork, and reserve for another use.

2. Add butter to pork drippings in Dutch oven over medium heat; whisk in cornmeal, and cook, whisking constantly, 1 minute. Add celery and next 4 ingredients; sauté 2 minutes.

3. Add broth and corncobs. Bring to a boil; reduce heat, and simmer 30 minutes. Remove and discard corncobs. Stir in crabmeat and next 4 ingredients; cook until thoroughly heated.

spicy coconut shrimp soup

makes 4 to 6 servings · hands-on time 55 min. · total time 55 min.

Thai chile pepper is optional here, but for those who enjoy a little extra heat, it will add a spicy finish to each serving.

souper tip

To prepare the ginger, use the edge of a metal spoon to scrape off the skin before slicing or grating. This method is less wasteful—and you can get around the bumps much easier. A paring knife works, too.

1   lb. unpeeled, medium-size raw shrimp (36/40 count)
1   Tbsp. grated fresh ginger
4   garlic cloves, minced
2   tsp. olive oil
4   cups vegetable broth
1   (13.5-oz.) can unsweetened coconut milk
2½ Tbsp. fish sauce
1   Tbsp. light brown sugar
1   Tbsp. fresh lime juice
2   tsp. red curry paste
1   (8-oz.) package sliced fresh mushrooms
1   medium-size red bell pepper, chopped
¼   cup fresh basil leaves
¼   cup chopped fresh cilantro
¼   cup sliced green onions
1   Thai chile pepper, seeded and minced (optional)

1. Peel shrimp; devein, if desired.

2. Sauté ginger and garlic in hot oil in a large Dutch oven over medium-high heat 1 to 2 minutes or until fragrant. Add broth and next 5 ingredients. Bring broth mixture to a boil, and reduce heat to medium. Add mushrooms and bell pepper, and cook, stirring often, 3 to 5 minutes or until crisp-tender. Add shrimp, and cook 1 to 2 minutes or just until shrimp turn pink. Remove from heat. Add basil, next 2 ingredients, and, if desired, chile pepper.

BUY IT RIGHT!

shrimp savvy

Use these tips for buying and storing shrimp when you are making a seafood soup.

Instead of peeling and deveining shrimp, you can buy it that way at the fish counter or the frozen foods section. Here's a guide for how much peeled and deveined shrimp to buy if your recipe calls for unpeeled shrimp. Or, if it calls for a specific amount of peeled, deveined shrimp and you prefer to buy it unpeeled, use this guide to purchase the correct amount.

Unpeeled Raw Shrimp	Peeled & Deveined Raw Shrimp
⅔ pound	½ pound
1 pound	¾ pound
1⅓ pounds	1 pound
2 pounds	1½ pounds
2⅔ pounds	2 pounds
4 pounds	3 pounds

The terms describing the size of shrimp like "small," "medium," "large," and "jumbo" are not regulated, and vary from store to store. The way to truly know the size of shrimp you are buying is by the number of shrimp you get per pound, or the "count." The fewer shrimp per pound, the larger and more expensive they are.

Here are some of the standard sizes you'll find:

- **61-70, 51-60:** Often labeled as "tiny," "extra small," or "small," these shrimp are good for shrimp salads.
- **43-50, 36-42:** Labeled as "medium" or "medium large," these shrimp are good for pasta dishes or mixed seafood dishes.
- **31-35, 26-30:** Often labeled as "large," these shrimp are readily available and can be used in a variety of shrimp dishes.
- **21-25, 16-20:** Often labeled "jumbo," these are a good choice when shrimp, prepared with few other ingredients, is the main course. For a main dish, each person might get 4-6 shrimp.
- **10-15, usually 10:** These shrimp may be referred to as "colossal" and can be considered an indulgence, as they are both expensive and impressive.

shrimp-cheese soup

makes 6 cups · hands-on time 15 min. · total time 45 min.

souper tip

That little black line that runs down the back of a shrimp (the sand vein) is its intestinal tract. In small shrimp, the vein is not really noticeable and often left in. But in larger shrimp, it looks less appealing and adds a slightly gritty texture. If it doesn't bother you, then there's no need to devein since it won't harm you.

If you'd prefer not to use wine, you can replace it with an equal amount of chicken broth in this recipe.

1   lb. unpeeled, jumbo raw shrimp (21/25 count)
1   Tbsp. butter
2   Tbsp. olive oil
1   medium onion, minced
1   to 2 garlic cloves, minced
1   cup dry white wine
1   (8-oz.) bottle clam juice
4   tomatoes, peeled and chopped
1   tsp. table salt
¾   tsp. dried oregano
½   tsp. freshly ground pepper
1   (4-oz.) package feta cheese, crumbled
¼   cup chopped fresh parsley

1. Peel shrimp, and devein, if desired.

2. Melt butter with oil in a Dutch oven over medium heat. Add onion and garlic; sauté 5 minutes. Add wine and next 5 ingredients; bring to a boil. Reduce heat, and simmer 10 minutes or until thickened. Stir in cheese, and simmer 10 minutes. Add shrimp, and cook 3 to 5 minutes or just until shrimp turn pink. Stir in parsley.

oyster bisque

makes about 7 cups · hands-on time 25 min. · total time 25 min.

....

2	pt. fresh oysters, undrained		1	tsp. table salt
¼	cup butter		1	tsp. black pepper
1	medium-size green bell pepper, chopped		⅛	tsp. ground nutmeg
1	medium onion, chopped		⅛	tsp. paprika
1	(8-oz.) package sliced fresh mushrooms		2	cups whipping cream
¼	cup all-purpose flour		¼	cup dry white wine or 2 Tbsp. dry sherry
				Oyster crackers

1. Drain oysters, reserving 1 cup liquid. Set oysters and liquid aside.

2. Melt butter in a Dutch oven over medium-high heat; add bell pepper and onion, and sauté 7 minutes or until tender. Add mushrooms, and sauté 5 minutes.

3. Stir in flour and next 4 ingredients. Reduce heat to medium, and cook, stirring constantly, 3 minutes. Gradually stir in reserved liquid and whipping cream; cook 5 minutes or until thickened and bubbly. Stir in oysters, and cook 3 minutes or until oysters begin to curl. Stir in wine. Serve with oyster crackers.

Pot Likker Soup,
page 53

meat
and
veggie
soups

peppered beef soup

makes 12 cups · hands-on time 20 min. · total time 8 hours, 28 min.

souper tip

Freeze leftovers in an airtight container up to three months. Add a bit of canned broth when reheating to reach desired consistency.

You can substitute 3 cups of low-sodium beef broth for the beer, if you like.

1   (4-lb.) sirloin tip beef roast
½   cup all-purpose flour
2   Tbsp. canola oil
1   medium-size red onion, thinly sliced
6   garlic cloves, minced
2   large baking potatoes, peeled and diced
1   (16-oz.) package baby carrots
2   (12-oz.) bottles lager beer

2   Tbsp. balsamic vinegar
2   Tbsp. Worcestershire sauce
2   Tbsp. dried parsley flakes
1   Tbsp. beef bouillon granules
1½ to 3 tsp. freshly ground black pepper
4   bay leaves
Toasted Bread Bowls (optional)

1. Rinse roast, and pat dry. Cut a 1-inch-deep cavity in the shape of an "X" on top of roast. (Do not cut all the way through roast.) Dredge roast in flour; shake off excess.

2. Cook roast in hot oil in a Dutch oven over medium-high heat 1 to 2 minutes on each side or until lightly browned.

3. Place roast in a 6-qt. slow cooker. Stuff cavity with red onion and garlic; top roast with potatoes and baby carrots. Pour beer, balsamic vinegar, and Worcestershire sauce into slow cooker. Sprinkle with parsley, bouillon, and ground pepper. Add bay leaves to liquid in slow cooker.

4. Cover and cook on LOW 7 to 8 hours or until fork-tender. Discard bay leaves. Shred roast using two forks. Season with salt to taste. Serve in Toasted Bread Bowls, if desired.

toasted bread bowls

makes 6 bowls · hands-on time 10 min. · total time 10 min.

6 (5- to 6-inch) artisan bread rounds*
Vegetable cooking spray

2 Tbsp. grated Parmesan cheese

1. Preheat oven to 350°. Cut ½ to 1½ inches from top of each bread round; scoop out centers, leaving a ½-inch-thick shell. Reserve soft centers for another use. Lightly coat bread shells and, if desired, cut sides of tops, with cooking spray. Place, cut sides up, on baking sheets. Sprinkle with cheese.

2. Bake at 350° for 8 to 10 minutes or until toasted.

* 6 (4-inch) hoagie rolls may be substituted.

souper tip

homemade croutons

You can make these easy homemade croutons with deliciously soft centers from the reserved bread from Toasted Bread Bowls. To make them, preheat the oven to 400°. Cut the reserved centers into 1-inch cubes; coat lightly with olive oil cooking spray. Place in a zip-top plastic bag; add 1 tsp. desired dried herbs or seasonings. Seal bag, and shake to coat. Spread bread cubes in a single layer on a baking sheet, and coat again with cooking spray. Bake at 400°, stirring occasionally, 7 to 9 minutes or until lightly toasted. Cool completely. Store in an airtight container for up to three days.

VARIATION: Stove-Top Homemade Croutons Prepare and season the bread cubes according to oven-method directions. Cook croutons, stirring occasionally, in a lightly greased skillet over medium-low heat 6 to 8 minutes or until cubes are lightly browned and crisp. Cool completely.

beef vegetable soup

makes 18 cups · hands-on time 15 min. · total time 1 hour, 30 min.

souper tip

For a twist, substitute any blend of mixed frozen vegetables that you like. Try broccoli, cauliflower, and carrots or a gumbo mixture.

An extra-large bouillon cube adds more flavor. If you don't have this size, you can use two regular cubes.

1½ lb. beef stew meat
1 Tbsp. olive oil
1 (32-oz.) bag frozen mixed vegetables (peas, carrots, green beans, and lima beans)
1 (15-oz.) can tomato sauce
1 (14.5-oz.) can diced Italian-style tomatoes

1 medium-size baking potato, peeled and diced
1 celery rib, chopped
1 medium onion, chopped
2 garlic cloves, minced
½ cup ketchup
1 extra-large chicken bouillon cube
½ tsp. pepper

1. Cook meat in hot oil over medium-high heat in a large Dutch oven 6 to 8 minutes or until browned.

2. Stir in frozen mixed vegetables, next 9 ingredients, and 1½ qt. water, stirring to loosen particles from bottom of Dutch oven. Bring mixture to a boil over medium-high heat; cover, reduce heat to low, and simmer, stirring occasionally, 55 to 60 minutes or until potatoes are tender.

Note: We tested with Knorr Chicken Bouillon cubes.

steak soup

makes 16 cups · hands-on time 30 min. · total time 8 hours, 30 min.

1 (2-lb.) package top round steak, cut into 1-inch cubes
⅓ cup all-purpose flour
3 Tbsp. vegetable oil
5 baking potatoes, cut into ½-inch cubes
3 carrots, sliced
2 small onions, chopped
1 celery rib, chopped
1 cup frozen sweet green peas
1 (16-oz.) can whole kernel corn, drained
1 (6-oz.) can tomato paste
2 Tbsp. beef bouillon granules
1 to 2 tsp. pepper

1. Toss together steak and flour.

2. Brown steak in hot oil in a large skillet over medium-high heat 5 to 6 minutes.

3. Place steak, 4 cups water, and remaining ingredients in a 5-qt. slow cooker; stir. Cover and cook on HIGH 8 hours or until vegetables are tender.

souper tip

Round steak is an economical cut of beef. Browning the meat first and cooking it for a long time delivers the most tender results.

slow-cooker solutions

A slow cooker can be a cook's best friend. Follow these tricks for making the most of it.

1. Make-ahead magic. If your slow cooker has a removable insert, you can assemble the ingredients in the insert the night before for some recipes, and then refrigerate the whole thing. Keep in mind that starting with cold ingredients may increase the cook time.

2. Don't get burned. Although cooking time is more flexible in a slow cooker than in an oven, overcooking is possible, so test for doneness close to the time given in the recipe.

3. Thaw beforehand. Defrost any frozen foods before cooking a dish that includes meat, poultry, or seafood. This ensures that the contents of the insert reach a safe internal temperature quickly.

4. Remember time conversions. One hour on HIGH equals approximately 2 hours on LOW.

5. Cut uniform pieces. When cutting meat or vegetables, be sure the pieces are the same size so they cook evenly.

6. Trim the fat. Slow cooking requires little fat, so be sure to trim excess fat and skin from meats and poultry.

7. Don't stir things up. There's no need to stir ingredients unless a recipe specifically calls for it. Just layer the ingredients as the recipe directs.

8. You won't need much liquid. Use only the amount of liquid specified in the recipe.

9. Lay it on thick. You can thicken the juices and make gravy by removing the lid and cooking on HIGH for the last 20 to 30 minutes.

10. Fill it properly. Fill your slow cooker at least half full but no more than two-thirds full. This helps meat, poultry, and seafood reach a safe internal temperature quickly and cook evenly.

taco soup

makes 14 cups · hands-on time 25 min. · total time 55 min.

This is the ideal soup to feed a crowd or for a quick weeknight supper for your family. Most of the ingredients are pantry staples, so you'll be able to put together this meal quickly. You can prepare Quick Quesadillas on page 209 to serve alongside it.

1   lb. ground beef
2   (16-oz.) cans pinto beans, drained and rinsed
1   (16-oz.) package frozen cut green beans
1   (15-oz.) can ranch beans, undrained
1   (14.5-oz.) can stewed tomatoes
1   (14.5-oz.) can petite diced tomatoes, undrained
1   (12-oz.) package frozen whole kernel corn
1   (12-oz.) bottle beer*
1   (1-oz.) envelope taco seasoning mix
1   (1-oz.) envelope Ranch dressing mix
Toppings: corn chips, shredded Cheddar cheese

1. Brown ground beef in a large Dutch oven over medium-high heat, stirring constantly, 8 to 10 minutes or until meat crumbles and is no longer pink; drain. Return to Dutch oven.

2. Stir pinto beans, next 8 ingredients, and 2 cups water into beef; bring to a boil. Reduce heat to medium-low. Simmer, stirring occasionally, 30 minutes. Serve with desired toppings.

* 1½ cups chicken broth may be substituted.

pork dumpling soup

makes 5 servings · hands-on time 30 min. · total time 50 min.

The hoisin sauce in this recipe gives it a nice sweet-and-spicy kick.

½ lb. lean ground pork
1   Tbsp. minced fresh ginger
3   Tbsp. chopped fresh cilantro
3   Tbsp. hoisin sauce, divided
15 wonton wrappers

3   (14-oz.) cans low-sodium fat-free chicken broth
½   cup sliced fresh mushrooms
¼   cup sliced green onions
Garnish: cilantro leaves

souper tip

If you do not see ground pork in the meat case, ask the butcher to grind ½ lb. of boneless pork chops for this recipe.

1. Brown pork with ginger in a nonstick skillet over medium-high heat, stirring often, 5 minutes or until meat crumbles and is no longer pink.

2. Combine pork mixture, cilantro, and 2 Tbsp. hoisin sauce in a medium bowl.

3. Arrange 1 wonton wrapper on a clean, flat surface. (Cover remaining wrappers with a damp towel to prevent drying out.) Moisten edges of wrapper with water. Spoon about 1 Tbsp. pork mixture in center of wrapper; fold 2 opposite corners together over pork mixture, forming a triangle. Press edges together to seal. Cover with a damp cloth. Repeat procedure with remaining wrappers and pork mixture.

4. Bring broth and remaining 1 Tbsp. hoisin sauce to a light boil in a Dutch oven over medium heat; gently stir in 8 dumplings. Cook 4 to 5 minutes or until dumplings float to top. Place dumplings in 5 individual serving bowls. Repeat procedure with remaining 7 dumplings.

5. Add mushrooms and onions to simmering broth; cook 1 minute. Ladle 1 cup broth mixture over dumplings in bowls. Serve immediately.

pot likker soup

makes 6 to 8 servings · hands-on time 15 min. · total time 6 hours, 15 min.

Pot likker is the juice left in a pot after collards cook and is traditionally valued as a delicacy. Be sure to sop up the vitamin-rich pot likker with your cornbread.

1 Tbsp. olive oil
2 cups refrigerated prechopped onion
½ cup chopped carrot
2 garlic cloves, minced
1 (1-lb.) ham hock
4 (1-lb.) packages fresh collard greens, cleaned, trimmed, and chopped
½ tsp. table salt
½ tsp. freshly ground black pepper
¼ tsp. crushed red pepper
1 (32-oz.) container chicken broth

1. Heat oil in a large skillet over medium-high heat; add onion and carrot, and sauté 4 minutes or until tender. Add garlic; sauté 1 minute. Place vegetables, 4 cups water, ham hock, and remaining ingredients in a 5- to 6-qt. slow cooker. Cover and cook on HIGH 1 hour. Reduce heat to LOW, and cook 5 hours or until ham falls off the bone. Remove ham hock from slow cooker. Remove ham from bone, discarding bone. Chop ham, and stir into soup.

ham-and-bean soup

makes 8 servings · hands-on time 15 min. · total time 1 hour, 14 min.

souper tip

If you have leftover holiday ham, this soup is a tasty way to use it. You'll need about 2 cups to replace the ham steak called for in the recipe. Don't forget to toss in the bone for added flavor.

For extra color and texture, stir in 1 (5-oz.) package of fresh baby spinach just before serving. The heat of the soup will wilt it. You can use regular spinach if you like; just remove the stems before stirring it in.

1	(16-oz.) lean ham steak	2	(15-oz.) cans navy beans, drained
2	Tbsp. olive oil		
1	large onion, diced	2	(15-oz.) cans cannellini beans, drained
1	bunch green onions, chopped		
		1	(15½-oz.) can black-eyed peas, drained
2	large carrots, diced		
2	celery ribs, diced	4	large Yukon gold potatoes, peeled and diced (about 2 lb.)
1	Tbsp. jarred ham-flavored soup base		
½	tsp. pepper		**Garnish: Potato Leaves**

1. Trim fat from ham steak; coarsely chop ham. Reserve bone.

2. Cook ham in hot oil in a Dutch oven over medium-high heat, stirring often, 6 to 8 minutes or until browned. Add diced onion and next 5 ingredients, and sauté 5 minutes or until onion is tender.

3. Stir in reserved ham bone, navy beans, and next 3 ingredients; add water to cover. Bring to a boil; cover, reduce heat to low, and cook, stirring occasionally, 45 minutes. Remove and discard bone before serving.

potato leaves

makes about 20 leaves · hands-on time 15 min. · total time 20 min.

To make these colorful chips ahead, prepare the recipe as directed, and then place the cooked leaves in a single layer in a jelly-roll pan. Freeze the leaves on the pan until firm, and then transfer them to a zip-top plastic freezer bag. To reheat, place the leaves in a single layer on a lightly greased baking sheet, and bake them at 350° for 8 to 10 minutes or until thoroughly heated.

1 large sweet potato (about 12 oz.)

1 large Yukon gold potato (about 8 oz.)

½ cup canola oil

1. Cut potatoes into ⅛-inch-thick slices, placing slices in a large bowl of ice water as you work to prevent discoloration.

2. Cut potato slices into leaves, using assorted 2- to 3-inch leaf-shaped cutters. Return leaves to ice water until ready to use.

3. Drain potato leaves, and dry well with paper towels. Cook potato leaves, in batches, in hot oil in a large skillet over medium-high heat 1 minute on each side or until golden brown. Season with salt to taste.

white bean-and-collard soup

makes 12 cups · hands-on time 30 min. · total time 1 hour, 45 min.

....

2 thick hickory-smoked bacon slices	1 Tbsp. chicken bouillon granules
2 cups chopped smoked ham	1 tsp. ground chipotle chile pepper
1 medium onion, finely chopped	½ tsp. dried thyme
5 (16-oz.) cans navy beans, undrained	½ tsp. freshly ground pepper
1 cup barbecue sauce	3 cups shredded collard greens
1 (6-oz.) can tomato paste	Hot sauce

1. Cook bacon in a large Dutch oven over medium-high heat 4 to 5 minutes or until crisp; remove bacon, and drain on paper towels, reserving 2 Tbsp. drippings in Dutch oven. Crumble bacon.

2. Sauté ham and onion in hot drippings 10 minutes or until tender.

3. Add beans, next 6 ingredients, and 8 cups water. Bring to a boil over medium-high heat. Cover, reduce heat to medium-low, and simmer, stirring occasionally, 1 hour. Stir in collards; cook 10 minutes or until tender. Serve with crumbled bacon and hot sauce.

hearty italian soup with parmesan-pepper cornbread biscotti

makes 12 cups · hands-on time 40 min. · total time 2 hours, 40 min.

1 (16-oz.) package mild Italian sausage
2 tsp. olive oil
1 large onion, diced
2 garlic cloves, minced
1 (48-oz.) container chicken broth
2 (15-oz.) cans cannellini beans, drained and rinsed
2 (14.5-oz.) cans diced tomatoes
1 tsp. dried Italian seasoning
1 (5-oz.) package baby spinach
¼ cup fresh parsley leaves
¼ cup fresh basil
Freshly shaved Parmesan cheese

1. Cook sausage in hot oil in a Dutch oven over medium heat 7 to 8 minutes on each side or until browned. Remove sausage from Dutch oven, reserving drippings in Dutch oven. Sauté onion in hot drippings 3 minutes or until tender. Add garlic, and sauté 1 minute. Cut sausage into ¼-inch-thick slices, and return to Dutch oven.

2. Stir chicken broth and next 3 ingredients into sausage mixture; bring to a boil over medium-high heat. Reduce heat to medium-low, and simmer 25 minutes.

3. Stir in spinach and next 2 ingredients; cook, stirring occasionally, 5 to 6 minutes or until spinach is wilted. Top each serving with Parmesan cheese.

HOW TO:
prepare beans

Both canned and dried beans can provide hearty texture and flavor to soups. They're also a great source of protein and fiber.

get canned

Canned beans are a convenient choice and can be substituted in recipes that call for dried, but keep in mind that the sodium is higher than dried. You can reduce the sodium by 40 percent by rinsing and draining the canned beans, but even then, you might want to decrease the amount of salt in the recipe. If you need to limit the sodium in your diet, look for no-salt-added canned beans or organic beans, which tend to be lower in sodium than regular beans.

Here are some substitution amounts if you are using canned in place of dried beans:
• 1 lb. dried beans (2 to 2½ cups) = 4½ to 5 cups cooked beans
• 1 cup dried beans = 2 to 2½ cups cooked beans
• 1 (15-oz.) can beans = 1¾ to 2 cups

tips for tenderness

When preparing dried beans, follow these tips:
• Soak the beans before cooking them in your recipe.
• Do not add ingredients such as lemon juice, vinegar, tomatoes, chili sauce, ketchup, molasses, or wine until after the beans have been soaked and are fully cooked. Adding acidic ingredients or ingredients that are rich in calcium too early in the cooking process can prevent the beans from becoming tender.
• Add salt just before serving to avoid toughening bean skins.

cook dried beans

1. If you use dried beans in a recipe, you'll need to soak them first to reduce the cooking time and help them get tender. There are two methods of soaking: quick soaking and overnight soaking.

2. Place the beans in a large Dutch oven, and add cool water to 2 inches above the beans. For a quick soak, bring the beans to a boil, and cook for 2 minutes. Remove the pan from the heat; cover and let stand 1 hour before draining. For an overnight soak, cover the Dutch oven, let stand for 8 hours or overnight, and then drain.

3. Place the drained soaked beans back in the large Dutch oven. Add water to 2 inches above the beans, and bring to a boil; make sure the beans stay covered with the liquid the entire time they are cooking.

4. Partially cover the pan, reduce the heat, and simmer until the beans are tender. Skim the foam from the surface of the cooking liquid as needed. It's important to cook the beans at a simmer, not a boil, since boiling can cook the beans too quickly and cause the skins to split.

5. Taste the beans to make sure they're tender. Don't just go by the estimated cooking times since older beans and those cooked in hard water will take longer to cook.

peasant soup

makes 2½ qt. · hands-on time 35 min. · total time 2 hours, 5 min.

....

You may cook the first 6 ingredients and 4 cans chicken broth in a 5-qt. slow cooker on LOW for 4 hours. Add the remaining can of broth, coleslaw, and remaining ingredients, and then cook on HIGH 1 hour.

9	baby carrots, sliced
1	large onion, coarsely chopped
2	celery ribs, diced
¼	cup chopped fresh parsley
1	(16-oz.) package kielbasa sausage, cut into ¼-inch-thick slices*
1	bay leaf
5	(14½-oz.) cans chicken broth, divided
½	(10-oz.) package angel hair coleslaw
2	russet potatoes, peeled and cut into ½-inch cubes
½	cup frozen cut green beans
1	(15-oz.) can kidney beans, drained and rinsed
¼	tsp. dried thyme
½	tsp. pepper

1. Bring first 6 ingredients and 4 cans chicken broth to a boil in a stockpot; reduce heat, and simmer 45 minutes.

2. Add remaining broth, coleslaw, and remaining ingredients; simmer 30 minutes or until vegetables are tender. Remove and discard bay leaf. (Freeze leftover soup up to 1 month.)

*1 lb. coarsely chopped cooked ham may be substituted for kielbasa.

spiced butternut-pumpkin soup

makes 15 cups · hands-on time 45 min. · total time 1 hour, 35 min.

....

If you'd rather, you can substitute 3 pounds of butternut squash for 1¾ pounds of butternut squash and 1¾ pounds of pumpkin.

2   Tbsp. butter
1   large sweet onion, diced
1   large red bell pepper, chopped
3   garlic cloves, minced
2   Tbsp. finely grated fresh ginger
1   medium-size butternut squash, peeled and cubed (about 1¾ lb.)
1   small pumpkin, peeled and cubed (about 1¾ lb.)
1   large sweet potato, peeled and cubed
1   large Granny Smith apple, peeled and cubed
1   (32-oz.) container low-sodium chicken broth
2   bay leaves
1½ tsp. red curry paste*
½   tsp. ground pepper
¾   cup whipping cream
1   Tbsp. fresh lime juice

1. Melt butter in a large Dutch oven over medium-high heat; add onion and bell pepper, and sauté 8 minutes or until onion is golden. Stir in garlic and ginger, and cook 1 minute. Add squash, next 7 ingredients, and 4 cups water. Bring to a boil, reduce heat to medium-low, and simmer 20 minutes or until vegetables are tender. Remove from heat, and let stand 30 minutes, stirring occasionally. Remove and discard bay leaves.

2. Process soup, in batches, in a blender until smooth. Return to Dutch oven, and stir in cream. Bring to a simmer over medium heat; stir in lime juice, and season with salt and pepper to taste.

* 1 tsp. curry powder may be substituted.

baby carrot soup

makes 5 cups · hands-on time 10 min. · total time 45 min.

Smoky adobo sauce gives this creamy soup
a subtle touch of heat.

1   (7-oz.) can chipotle
    peppers in adobo sauce
1   small sweet onion,
    chopped
1   Tbsp. olive oil
1   (32-oz.) container low-
    sodium fat-free chicken
    broth

1   (16-oz.) package baby
    carrots
⅓   cup half-and-half
1   tsp. table salt
Toppings: chopped fresh
    chives, chopped dried
    chile peppers, sour cream

1. Remove 2 tsp. adobo sauce from can; reserve peppers and remaining
sauce for another use.

2. Sauté onion in hot oil in a Dutch oven over medium heat 3 to 4 minutes
or until tender. Stir in broth, carrots, and 2 tsp. adobo sauce; cover,
increase heat to medium-high, and bring to a boil. Reduce heat to
medium, and simmer, partially covered, 15 to 20 minutes or until carrots
are tender. Remove from heat, and let cool 10 minutes.

3. Process carrot mixture in a blender or food processor 1 minute or until
smooth, stopping to scrape down sides as needed. Return carrot mixture
to Dutch oven. Stir in half-and-half and salt. Cook over low heat 2 to 4
minutes or until thoroughly heated. Serve with desired toppings.

tomato-basil bisque

makes about 7 cups · hands-on time 15 min. · total time 15 min.

souper tip

Serve either of these rich tomato soups with grilled cheese sand-wiches. Choose thick artisanal breads and a variety of cheeses. Try Gouda, spicy Pepper Jack, or velvety Havarti. Heat your skillet or griddle over medium heat. You want the surface hot enough to brown the bread and melt the cheese without burning it.

2 (10¾-oz.) cans tomato soup, undiluted
1 (14½-oz.) can diced tomatoes
2½ cups buttermilk
2 Tbsp. chopped fresh basil
¼ tsp. freshly ground pepper
Toppings: fresh basil leaves, freshly ground pepper, grated Parmesan cheese

1. Cook first 5 ingredients in a 3-qt. saucepan over medium heat, stirring often, 6 to 8 minutes or until thoroughly heated. Serve immediately with desired toppings.

tomato soup with okra

makes 15 cups · hands-on time 10 min. · total time 1 hour, 10 min.

2 medium onions, chopped
4 Tbsp. olive oil, divided
3 (35-oz.) cans Italian-style whole peeled tomatoes with basil
1 (32-oz.) can chicken broth
1 cup loosely packed fresh basil leaves

3 garlic cloves
1 tsp. lemon zest
1 Tbsp. lemon juice
1 tsp. table salt
1 tsp. sugar
½ tsp. pepper
1 (16-oz.) package frozen breaded cut okra

1. Sauté onion in 2 Tbsp. hot oil in a large Dutch oven over medium-high heat 9 to 10 minutes or until tender. Add tomatoes and chicken broth. Bring to a boil; reduce heat to medium-low, and simmer, stirring occasionally, 20 minutes. Process mixture with a handheld blender until smooth.

2. Process basil, next 4 ingredients, ¼ cup water, and remaining 2 Tbsp. oil in a food processor until smooth, stopping to scrape down sides. Stir basil mixture, sugar, and pepper into soup. Cook 10 minutes or until thoroughly heated.

3. Meanwhile, cook okra according to package directions. Serve with soup.

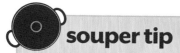

souper tip

For really crisp okra: Thaw frozen okra. Pour oil to a depth of 2 inches in a Dutch oven or cast-iron skillet; heat to 375°. Fry okra, in batches, 2 to 4 minutes or until golden; drain on paper towels.

sweet potato soup

makes 8 cups · hands-on time 40 min. · total time 1 hour

Make the soup through Step 2 the day before. Reheat, and stir in the lime juice before serving.

2 Tbsp. butter
1 medium onion, chopped
2 garlic cloves, minced
5½ cups reduced-sodium fat-free chicken broth
2 lb. sweet potatoes, peeled and chopped (2 large)
1 cup apple cider
1 tsp. minced canned chipotle pepper in adobo sauce
1 tsp. salt
2 Tbsp. fresh lime juice
½ cup sour cream
2 tsp. fresh lime juice
Garnish: cilantro leaves

1. Melt butter in a large saucepan over medium-high heat; add onion, and sauté 5 to 7 minutes or until tender. Add garlic; sauté 1 minute. Stir in broth and next 4 ingredients. Bring to a boil; reduce heat to medium-low, and simmer 20 minutes or until potatoes are tender.

2. Process mixture with a handheld blender until smooth. (If you don't have a handheld blender, cool mixture 10 minutes, and process, in batches, in a regular blender until smooth. Return to saucepan, and proceed with Step 3.)

3. Cook potato mixture over low heat, stirring occasionally, 5 minutes or until thoroughly heated. Stir in 2 Tbsp. lime juice. Whisk together sour cream and 2 tsp. lime juice. Ladle soup into bowls, and drizzle each serving with sour cream mixture.

loaded potato soup

makes 8 servings · hands-on time 15 min. · total time 5 hours, 35 min.

To get a head start on this soup, grate the cheese, cook and crumble the bacon, and slice the green onions in the morning. Store all the components in the refrigerator, and pull them out about 20 minutes before you serve the soup.

4   lb. new potatoes, peeled and cut into ¼-inch-thick slices
1   small onion, chopped
2   (14-oz.) cans chicken broth
2   tsp. table salt
½   tsp. pepper
1   pt. half-and-half
Toppings: shredded Cheddar cheese, crumbled cooked bacon, green onion slices

1. Layer sliced potatoes in a lightly greased 6-qt. slow cooker; top with chopped onion.

2. Stir together chicken broth, salt, and pepper; pour over potatoes and onion. (Broth will not completely cover potatoes and onion.) Cover and cook on HIGH 3 to 5 hours or until potatoes are tender. Mash mixture with a potato masher; stir in half-and-half. Cover and cook on HIGH 20 more minutes or until mixture is thoroughly heated. Ladle into bowls, and serve with desired toppings.

baked potato-and-broccoli soup

makes 7 servings · hands-on time 20 min. · total time 40 min.

souper tip

For the best results, shred the blocks of cheese (versus the pre-shredded variety) for additional creaminess and even melting.

¼ cup all-purpose flour
2 (14¼-oz.) cans low-sodium fat-free chicken broth, divided
3 cups peeled, cubed potato (about 1¼ lb.)
2 cups broccoli florets, chopped
1 small onion, chopped

1¼ cups 2% reduced-fat milk
1 (8-oz.) block 2% reduced-fat sharp Cheddar cheese, shredded
7 tsp. shredded 2% reduced-fat sharp Cheddar cheese
7 tsp. fully cooked bacon pieces
7 tsp. chopped green onions

1. Whisk together flour and ⅓ cup chicken broth until smooth.

2. Combine remaining chicken broth and next 3 ingredients in a Dutch oven. Bring to a boil; cover, reduce heat, and simmer 8 minutes or until potatoes are tender. Gradually stir in flour mixture. Cook, stirring often, 5 minutes.

3. Stir in milk and 8 oz. shredded cheese. Cook mixture over medium-low heat, stirring constantly, until cheese melts. Top each serving of soup with 1 tsp. cheese, 1 tsp. bacon pieces, and 1 tsp. chopped green onions.

cream of mushroom soup

makes 5 cups · hands-on time 25 min. · total time 25 min.

This makes 5 cups, about the same as four 10.75-oz. cans. Use 1¼ cups of this in place of each can called for in your recipe.

½ cup butter, divided
3 (8-oz.) packages fresh mushrooms, chopped
⅓ cup all-purpose flour
2 cups whipping cream
1 (8-oz.) package cream cheese, softened
2 (1-oz.) containers home-style concentrated chicken stock (from a 4.66-oz. package)

1. Melt 3 Tbsp. butter in a Dutch oven over medium-high heat; add mushrooms, and sauté 10 to 12 minutes or until liquid evaporates. Transfer to a bowl.

2. Reduce heat to medium. Melt remaining 5 Tbsp. butter in Dutch oven. Whisk in flour until smooth; whisk 1 minute. Gradually whisk in cream and next 2 ingredients. Cook, whisking constantly, 2 minutes or until melted and smooth. Remove from heat; stir in mushrooms. Use immediately, or cool completely. Freeze in 1¼-cup portions in plastic freezer bags. Thaw before using.

Note: We tested with Knorr Homestyle Concentrated Stock.

cheddar cheese soup

makes 8 cups · hands-on time 25 min. · total time 35 min.

The cheese soup gets a slight kick from ground red pepper. To complete the meal, serve this soup with a simple sandwich: Layer guacamole, tomato slices lightly sprinkled with salt and pepper, bacon slices, and arugula on whole-grain bread slices.

¼ cup butter
½ cup finely chopped carrots
½ cup finely chopped celery
1 small onion, finely chopped
½ small green bell pepper, finely chopped
2 garlic cloves, minced
⅓ cup all-purpose flour
1 extra-large chicken bouillon cube
2 cups milk
1 (8-oz.) block sharp Cheddar cheese, shredded
¼ tsp. ground red pepper

1. Melt butter in a 3-qt. saucepan over medium-high heat; add carrots and next 4 ingredients, and sauté 5 to 7 minutes or until tender. Sprinkle flour over vegetable mixture, and stir until coated. Stir in bouillon cube, milk, and 3 cups water; cook, stirring occasionally, 10 to 11 minutes or until mixture is slightly thickened and bubbly.

2. Add shredded cheese and red pepper, stirring until well blended. Serve immediately.

red lentil soup

makes 11 cups · hands-on time 25 min. · total time 55 min.

souper tip

Unlike other dried legumes, lentils need no pre-soaking and cook much more quickly. Be sure to start tasting the lentils for desired tenderness 10 to 15 minutes before the end of the cooking time. If you overcook them, they'll become mushy.

You can top this soup with additional fresh basil leaves, if you like. Pair it with a hearty sandwich: Layer chutney, Havarti cheese slices, deli pork slices, and Dijon mustard between multigrain bread slices. Spread the outside of the sandwiches with butter; cook on a hot griddle over medium heat for 3 minutes on each side or until lightly browned.

2	Tbsp. butter	2	cups dried red lentils
1	sweet onion, diced	2	extra-large chicken bouillon cubes
1	cup chopped carrots		
1	cup chopped celery	½	tsp. ground cumin
4	garlic cloves, minced	½	tsp. table salt
1	(28-oz.) can diced tomatoes	¼	tsp. pepper
		1	cup chopped fresh basil

1. Melt butter in a Dutch oven over medium-high heat. Add onion and next 3 ingredients, and sauté 5 to 6 minutes or until tender. Add tomatoes, next 5 ingredients, and 5 cups water.

2. Bring to a boil; reduce heat to medium, and cook, stirring occasionally, 30 minutes or until lentils are tender. Stir in basil just before serving.

hoppin' john soup

makes 11 cups · hands-on time 30 min. · total time 2 hours, 5 min.

Bestow good luck on New Year's Day with this hearty recipe. Smoky flavor runs throughout this soup of peas and collards. When choosing collards, look for crisp greens with even color. Avoid wilted or yellowing ones.

½   (16-oz.) package dried black-eyed peas, rinsed and sorted
2   lb. smoked turkey wings
⅓   cup finely chopped country ham
¼   tsp. dried crushed red pepper
2   garlic cloves, minced
1   jalapeño pepper, seeded and minced
2   carrots, cut into 1-inch pieces

1   celery rib, diced
1   large sweet onion, diced
1   bay leaf
2   Tbsp. canola oil
½   (16-oz.) package fresh collard greens, trimmed and finely chopped
1   Tbsp. hot sauce
1   Tbsp. apple cider vinegar
Hot cooked brown rice
Jalapeño Cornbread Croutons
Fresh flat-leaf parsley leaves

1. Bring peas, turkey wings, and 6 cups water to a boil in a large Dutch oven. Cover, reduce heat to medium, and simmer 45 minutes or until peas are tender, skimming any foam from surface. Drain peas, reserving 1¼ cups liquid. Remove turkey meat from bones. Chop meat.

2. Sauté ham and next 7 ingredients in hot oil in Dutch oven over medium-high heat 10 minutes or until vegetables are tender. Add peas, reserved 1¼ cups liquid, turkey meat, collards, hot sauce, and 6 cups water. Bring to a boil; reduce heat to medium, and simmer, stirring occasionally, 30 minutes. Stir in vinegar. Season with salt and pepper. Remove and discard bay leaf. Serve over rice with cornbread croutons and parsley.

jalapeño cornbread croutons

makes 6 dozen using a 9-inch pan (yield depends on pan size)
hands-on time 7 min. · total time 39 min.

· ·

1 **(6-oz.) package buttermilk
   cornbread-and-muffin mix**
½ **cup chopped fresh cilantro**

2 **jalapeño peppers, seeded
   and chopped**

1. Prepare batter according to package directions. Stir in cilantro and jalapeño peppers. Pour batter into a 9-inch baking pan, and bake according to package directions. Cool on a wire rack 10 minutes. Cut into 1-inch cubes.

2. Preheat oven to 375° and bake in a single layer in a lightly greased jelly-roll pan until edges are golden, stirring halfway through.

maque choux soup

makes 6 cups · hands-on time 40 min. · total time 40 min.

Pronounced "mock shoe," this Louisiana staple (which is like a succotash) is a Cajun take on a Native American dish. Run a knife along just-cut cobs to catch sweet corn milk in a bowl. It'll add flavor and creamy texture.

3   cups fresh corn kernels (about 6 ears)
1   medium-size orange bell pepper, chopped
¼   tsp. ground cumin
¼   tsp. ground coriander
1   (32-oz.) container chicken broth
¾   tsp. kosher salt
½   tsp. freshly ground black pepper
½   cup sour cream
3   Tbsp. plain white cornmeal
Toppings: cooked bacon pieces, fresh flat-leaf parsley leaves, fresh lime juice

souper tip

To prepare corn for Maque Choux Soup, cut tips of corn kernels, using a paring knife. Scrape milk and pulp from cob into a bowl.

1. Stir together corn and bell pepper. Place a large cast-iron skillet over medium-high heat until hot. Add half of corn mixture; cook, stirring constantly, 4 minutes or until vegetables begin to char. Transfer mixture to a 3-qt. saucepan. Add remaining corn mixture to skillet; cook, stirring constantly, 4 minutes or until vegetables begin to char. Stir in cumin and coriander; cook, stirring constantly, 2 to 3 minutes or until fragrant.

2. Add 2 cups broth to corn mixture in saucepan, and process with a handheld blender 1 to 2 minutes or until slightly smooth. Add remaining corn mixture and 2 cups broth to saucepan; bring to a light boil over medium heat. Reduce heat to medium-low, and simmer, stirring often, 5 minutes. Stir in salt and pepper.

3. Whisk together sour cream and cornmeal in a heatproof bowl. Whisk in ½ cup hot soup. Add sour cream mixture to soup. Simmer, stirring occasionally, 5 minutes or until thickened. Serve with desired toppings.

vegetable soup with basil pesto

makes about 10 cups · hands-on time 20 min. · 'total time 42 min.

- 2 medium carrots, chopped
- 2 celery ribs, chopped
- 1 large sweet onion, chopped
- 4 garlic cloves, minced
- 1 tsp. minced fresh thyme
- 1 Tbsp. olive oil
- 2 (32-oz.) containers organic vegetable broth
- 2 plum tomatoes, seeded and chopped
- 1 medium zucchini, chopped
- 1¼ tsp. kosher salt
- ½ tsp. freshly ground black pepper
- 1 (15-oz.) can cannellini beans, drained and rinsed
- ½ cup uncooked mini farfalle (bow-tie) pasta
- Basil Pesto

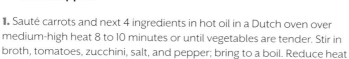

souper tip

If you're short on time, reach for a good-quality refrigerated pesto at the supermarket to substitute for this homemade blend. You can also use this pesto to dress up canned soups, spread on pizza, or brush on grilled vegetables.

1. Sauté carrots and next 4 ingredients in hot oil in a Dutch oven over medium-high heat 8 to 10 minutes or until vegetables are tender. Stir in broth, tomatoes, zucchini, salt, and pepper; bring to a boil. Reduce heat to medium-low, and simmer, stirring occasionally, 10 minutes.

2. Stir in beans and pasta, and cook, stirring occasionally, 10 to 12 minutes or until pasta is tender. Top each serving with 1 to 2 tsp. Basil Pesto.

basil pesto

makes about ½ cup · hands-on time 5 min. · total time 5 min.

- 2 cups firmly packed fresh basil leaves
- ½ cup (2 oz.) grated Parmesan cheese
- 3 Tbsp. extra virgin olive oil
- 1 garlic clove, chopped
- ½ tsp. kosher salt

1. Process all ingredients in a food processor until finely ground. Refrigerate in an airtight container up to 1 week.

caramelized onion soup with swiss cheese-and-basil croutons

makes 8 cups · hands-on time 20 min. · total time 1 hour, 9 min.

souper tip

A Dutch oven works best here for caramelizing the onions, but for smaller amounts (less than 4 cups), you can use a nonstick skillet coated with oil.

6	medium onions, halved and thinly sliced
¼	cup olive oil
4	garlic cloves, pressed
3	Tbsp. beef bouillon granules
1	tsp. pepper
1	tsp. chopped fresh thyme
2	Tbsp. dry sherry (optional)
1	(8-oz.) French baguette
1	cup (4 oz.) shredded Swiss cheese
2	Tbsp. chopped fresh basil
2	Tbsp. mayonnaise

1. Cook sliced onions in hot oil in a Dutch oven over medium-high heat, stirring occasionally, 20 to 25 minutes or until onions are golden brown. Add garlic, and cook 1 minute. Stir in 8 cups water, bouillon granules, pepper, and thyme. Add sherry, if desired. Cover, reduce heat to low, and simmer, stirring occasionally, 20 minutes.

2. Ladle soup into oven-safe serving bowls, and place on a baking sheet. Preheat broiler to HIGH.

3. Cut baguette diagonally into 8 slices. Stir together Swiss cheese, basil, and mayonnaise. Spread mixture evenly on 1 side of bread slices. Top soup with bread slices, cheese side up.

4. Broil 5 inches from heat 2½ to 3 minutes or until lightly browned. Serve immediately.

Playoff Chili,
page 103

chili
many
ways

easy beef chili

makes 2 qt. · hands-on time 35 min. · total time 55 min.

Rich, beefy petite tender is the quick-cooking foundation of this chili and a supermarket steak cut from shoulder. It looks and tastes like tenderloin but costs a third of the price. Can't find it? Try chuck-eye steak, which has good flavor but needs a little more trimming.

2   lb. beef petite tender steak (aka shoulder tender), trimmed and cut into 1-inch cubes
2   Tbsp. olive oil
1   yellow onion, chopped
4   garlic cloves, chopped
2   to 3 tsp. chipotle chile powder
2   tsp. dried oregano
2   tsp. ground cumin
1   (6-oz.) can tomato paste
5   (4.5-oz.) cans chopped green chiles
4   cups chicken broth
1   (14.5-oz.) can stewed tomatoes
2   Tbsp. plain yellow cornmeal

Toppings: sliced green onions, fried onion rings, sour cream, shredded Cheddar cheese

1. Sprinkle beef with desired amount of salt and pepper. Cook beef in hot oil in a large, enamel cast-iron Dutch oven over medium-high heat, stirring often, 5 to 6 minutes or until browned. Transfer beef to a platter.

2. Add onion to Dutch oven, and cook, stirring often, 3 minutes or until tender. Add garlic and next 3 ingredients; cook, stirring constantly, 2 minutes. Stir in tomato paste, and cook, stirring constantly, 2 minutes.

3. Add chiles, next 2 ingredients, beef, and 1 cup water; bring to a boil. Boil, stirring occasionally, 20 minutes. Add salt to taste. Sprinkle with cornmeal. Cook, stirring constantly, 5 minutes or until thickened. Serve with desired toppings.

chunky beef chili

makes 9 cups · hands-on time 25 min. · total time 1 hour, 55 min.

souper tip

If you've had spices longer than a year, it might be time to replace them. Seasonings tend to dull in flavor the longer they sit on the shelf. Always store them in a cool, dry place.

4 lb. boneless chuck roast, cut into ½-inch pieces
2 Tbsp. chili powder
2 (6-oz.) cans tomato paste
1 (32-oz.) container beef broth
2 (8-oz.) cans tomato sauce
2 tsp. granulated garlic
1 tsp. table salt
1 tsp. dried oregano
1 tsp. ground cumin
1 tsp. paprika
1 tsp. onion powder
½ tsp. ground black pepper
¼ tsp. ground red pepper
Texas Cornbread Sticks (page 192)
Toppings: crushed tortilla chips, sour cream, shredded Cheddar cheese, chopped onion

1. Brown meat, in batches, in a Dutch oven over medium-high heat. Remove meat, reserving drippings in Dutch oven. Add chili powder to Dutch oven; cook, stirring constantly, 2 minutes. Stir in tomato paste; cook 5 minutes.

2. Return beef to Dutch oven. Stir in beef broth and next 9 ingredients; bring to a boil. Reduce heat to low, and simmer, uncovered, stirring occasionally, 1½ hours or until beef is tender. Serve with Texas Cornbread Sticks, if desired, and desired toppings.

texas-style chili

makes about 8 cups · hands-on time 15 min. · total time 3 hours, 15 min.

- 1 (10½-oz.) can condensed chicken broth
- 4 dried ancho chile peppers, stemmed and seeded
- 2 Tbsp. all-purpose flour
- 1½ tsp. ground cumin
- 1 tsp. table salt
- 1 (2-lb.) London broil, cut into ½-inch cubes
- 2 chopped onions
- 4 garlic cloves, minced
- 1½ tsp. dried oregano
- 1 (16-oz.) bottle dark beer
- Halved jalapeño peppers
- Sour cream
- Refrigerated salsa
- Saltine crackers

1. Microwave broth in a microwave-safe bowl at HIGH 2 to 3 minutes or until simmering. Place ancho chile peppers in a blender. Pour hot broth over peppers; let stand 10 minutes. Holding lid down with a towel, process peppers and broth until smooth.

2. Sprinkle flour, cumin, and salt over London broil. Place beef in a 4-qt. slow cooker. Add chopped onions, minced garlic, oregano, beer, 1 cup water, and pepper mixture. Cover and cook on HIGH 3 to 4 hours (or on LOW 5 to 6 hours) or until beef is tender. Top with halved jalapeño peppers, sour cream, and refrigerated salsa. Serve with saltine crackers.

Note: We tested with Los Chileros de Nuevo Mexico whole ancho chiles.

souper tip

This chili is classified as Texas-style because it uses a beef roast and has no beans. Another Lone Star touch: adding a kick of flavor from reconstituted ancho chiles. An ancho is a dried poblano chile. It has mild to medium heat with a sweet, fruity flavor and hints of cherry, prune, and fig.

big-batch chili

makes 15 to 18 cups · hands-on time 20 min. · total time 6 hours

You can also prepare this on the stovetop: Cook the ground chuck, in batches, in a large Dutch oven, drain the beef, and return it to the Dutch oven. Add the onions, next 12 ingredients, and, if desired, beans. Bring to a boil over medium-high heat; then reduce the heat, cover, and simmer 4 to 6 hours. Be sure to remove and discard the bay leaf.

 **souper tip**

We're not kidding about this being a big batch of chili, but you can freeze it. Here's how: Let the chili stand 30 minutes. Evenly divide chili mixture into 3 (1-gallon) zip-top plastic freezer bags; seal and lay each bag flat. Stack the bags of chili in the freezer. You can freeze it for up to one month. To thaw, place the frozen chili in the refrigerator overnight or defrost it in the microwave. Pour thawed chili into a 9-inch square baking dish, cover tightly with heavy-duty plastic wrap, and fold back a corner to allow steam to escape. Microwave at HIGH 6 to 7 minutes or until bubbly, stirring after 3½ minutes.

4 lb. ground chuck
2 medium onions, chopped
1 green bell pepper, chopped
2 garlic cloves, minced
3 (14½-oz.) cans diced tomatoes, undrained
4 (8-oz.) cans tomato sauce
1 (6-oz.) can tomato paste
¼ cup chili powder
1 Tbsp. sugar
1 tsp. table salt

1 tsp. black pepper
½ tsp. paprika
½ tsp. ground red pepper
1 bay leaf
2 (16-oz.) cans light red kidney beans, drained and rinsed (optional)
Toppings: sour cream, shredded Cheddar cheese, chopped green onions, sliced ripe black olives

1. Cook ground chuck, in batches, in a large skillet over medium-high heat about 5 minutes, stirring until meat crumbles and is no longer pink; drain. Place meat in a 6-qt. slow cooker; stir in onions, next 12 ingredients, and, if desired, beans. Cover and cook on HIGH 5 to 6 hours or on LOW 6 to 8 hours. Remove and discard bay leaf. Serve with desired toppings.

TOP IT OFF!

do-it-yourself chili bar

Visual guide for a chili chow-down, letting folks doctor and spice to suit their own taste.

Cheeses

Monterey Jack: Can provide a little heat relief in really spicy chilis.

Pepper Jack: Will add spiciness to a milder chili.

Fontina: Adds a creamy and nutty, unexpected flavor.

Cheddar: Whether it is sharp, extra sharp, or white; this cheese melts well and can top any type of chili.

Queso fresco: Fresh Mexican-style cheese is a little salty and crumbly.

Peppers (fresh & ground)

Fresh bell peppers: Have a sweet, mild flavor and give a little crunch.

Fresh serrano peppers: Can be blistering hot to somewhat mild. Their size and shape make them difficult to core and seed, so the best way to control the heat is to use less of them.

Fresh jalapeño peppers: Actually vary from mild to hot. The heat is concentrated in the seeds and the veins, so if you want a milder taste, remove the seeds and veins.

Pickled jalapeño peppers: Remove from the jar with a slotted spoon, and serve. Heat can vary.

Canned diced chiles: These peppers are roasted, peeled and diced. They add a mild, slightly acidic flavor.

Red or cayenne peppers: They are hot and pungent; made from peppers that originated in French Guyana.

Chipotle peppers: Chipotles are ripe (red), dried, smoked jalapeños.

Black pepper: Freshly ground black peppercorns deliver the best flavor.

Other Favorites

Sour cream
Tabasco hot pepper sauce
Sriracha hot chili sauce
Cholula hot sauces
Diced tomatoes
Diced sweet and red onions
Sliced green onions
Fresh corn kernels
Chopped cilantro

mole chili

makes 4 servings · hands-on time 5 min. · total time 14 min.

souper tip

Chocolate is often added to savory Mexican dishes to cut the heat and enrich the flavor. In this recipe, chocolate adds richness and deepens the color of the chili without making it sweet.

1	lb. ground round
1	cup chopped onion (about 1 small onion)
1	garlic clove, minced
1	(14.5-oz.) can diced tomatoes with green chiles, undrained
1	(16-oz.) can pinto beans, drained and rinsed

2	Tbsp. chili powder
1	oz. semisweet chocolate, coarsely chopped
1	tsp. ground cumin
1	tsp. table salt
½	tsp. dried oregano
⅛	tsp. ground cinnamon

Toppings: sour cream, chopped fresh cilantro

1. Brown ground beef in a large Dutch oven over medium-high heat, stirring until meat crumbles and is no longer pink; drain. Return beef to pan. Add onion and garlic to pan; cook, stirring occasionally, 4 minutes or until tender. Add tomatoes, 1 cup water, and remaining 7 ingredients; cover and simmer 7 minutes. Serve immediately with desired toppings.

beefy corn-and-black bean chili

makes 6 servings · hands-on time 15 min. · total time 27 min.

This dish has the flavor and aroma of a chili that has simmered all day—only it hasn't. Dress it up with a dollop of sour cream and a sprinkle of sliced green onions.

1   lb. ground round
2   tsp. salt-free chili powder blend
1   (14-oz.) package frozen seasoned corn and black beans
1   (14-oz.) can beef broth
1   (15-oz.) can seasoned diced tomato sauce for chili
Toppings: sour cream, sliced green onions

1. Combine beef and chili powder blend in a large Dutch oven. Cook 6 minutes over medium-high heat or until beef is browned, stirring to crumble. Drain and return to pan.

2. Stir in frozen corn mixture, broth, and tomato sauce; bring to a boil. Cover, reduce heat, and simmer 10 minutes. Uncover and simmer 5 minutes, stirring occasionally. Serve with desired toppings.

Note: We tested with Hunt's Seasoned Diced Tomato Sauce for Chili.

beef-and-butternut squash chili

makes 6 to 8 servings · hands-on time 20 min. · total time 1 hour, 10 min.

1   lb. lean ground beef
1   green bell pepper,
    chopped
1   medium onion, chopped
2   garlic cloves, minced
2   (14.5-oz.) cans Mexican-
    style stewed tomatoes,
    chopped

1   (16-oz.) can chili beans
½   small butternut squash,
    peeled and cubed (about
    1½ cups)
1   cup low-sodium beef broth
1½ tsp. ground cumin
1½ tsp. chili powder
1   cup frozen corn kernels

1. Cook beef, bell pepper, and next 2 ingredients in a Dutch oven over medium-high heat until meat crumbles and is no longer pink. Drain well, and return to Dutch oven.

2. Stir in tomatoes and next 5 ingredients; bring to a boil over medium-high heat. Cover, reduce heat to medium-low, and simmer, stirring occasionally, 15 minutes. Stir in corn, and cook, uncovered, 15 minutes or until squash is tender and chili is thickened.

souper tip

This chili is loaded with beef and beans for zinc and B vitamins, tomatoes and green peppers for vitamin C, and butternut squash for beta-carotene.

playoff chili

makes 14 servings · hands-on time 25 min. · total time 2 hours, 40 min.

This chili freezes well. After it has cooled, transfer it to a zip-top plastic freezer bag. It'll keep for up to three months.

- 1 lb. ground beef
- 1 lb. ground pork
- 1 large white onion, chopped
- 1 large green bell pepper, seeded and chopped
- 1 large red bell pepper, seeded and chopped
- 2 garlic cloves, minced
- 1 (14½-oz.) can diced tomatoes with green chiles
- 1 (12-oz.) bottle beer
- 1 (8-oz.) can tomato sauce
- 1 Tbsp. chili powder
- 1 tsp. ground cumin
- 1 tsp. sugar
- 1 tsp. table salt
- ½ tsp. ground red pepper
- ½ tsp. black pepper
- ½ tsp. dried oregano
- 1 (16-oz.) can kidney beans, rinsed and drained
- 1 (16-oz.) can black beans, drained and rinsed

Garnishes: chopped onion, shredded Cheddar cheese, sour cream

1. Cook ground beef and next 5 ingredients in a Dutch oven over medium heat 10 minutes or until meat crumbles and is no longer pink. Stir in diced tomatoes with green chiles and next 9 ingredients, and bring to a boil. Cover, reduce heat to low, and simmer 1 hour and 45 minutes, stirring every 20 minutes. Add kidney beans and black beans; cover and cook 15 minutes.

superquick chili

makes 8 servings · hands-on time 12 min. · total time 27 min.

souper tip

To serve at a party, slice the tops from 16 (1-oz.) hearty round dinner rolls, hollow out centers, and then let guests spoon chili into them. Serve with a variety of toppings (see page 94 for ideas) so everyone can customize theirs.

2   lb. lean ground beef
2   Tbsp. chili powder
1   Tbsp. Creole seasoning
1   tsp. ground cumin
2   (16-oz.) cans diced tomatoes with green pepper and onion
2   (16-oz.) cans small red beans, undrained
2   (8-oz.) cans tomato sauce
Toppings: shredded Cheddar cheese, sliced green onions, diced tomatoes

1. Brown beef in a Dutch oven over medium-high heat, stirring often, 6 to 8 minutes or until beef crumbles and is no longer pink; drain well. Return beef to Dutch oven; sprinkle with chili powder, Creole seasoning, and cumin, and sauté 1 minute.

2. Stir in diced tomatoes and next 2 ingredients, and bring to a boil over medium-high heat, stirring occasionally. Cover, reduce heat to low, and simmer, stirring occasionally, 15 minutes. Serve with desired toppings.

pork chili

makes 6 servings · hands-on time 10 min. · total time 55 min.

Off-the-shelf ingredients make this crowd-pleasing dish a snap to prepare. Serve with your favorite taco toppings, and let guests help themselves.

½ cup all-purpose flour
3 Tbsp. chili powder
2 tsp. table salt
1½ tsp. ground cumin
2 lb. boneless pork loin, cut into 1-inch cubes
2 Tbsp. canola oil
1 large onion, diced
4 garlic cloves, minced
2 (16-oz.) cans kidney beans, undrained

2 (16-oz.) cans whole kernel white corn, drained
2 (10-oz.) cans diced tomatoes and green chiles with lime juice and cilantro, undrained
2 (4.5-oz.) cans chopped green chiles, undrained

souper tip

When cooking bite-size pieces of meat, consider cooking in batches to avoid steaming the meat instead of browning it. Allow the meat to brown on one side before turning. Remove the batches using a slotted spoon, and keep the meat warm.

1. Stir together first 4 ingredients. Reserve 2 Tbsp. flour mixture. Dredge pork in remaining flour mixture.

2. Cook pork in hot oil in a Dutch oven over medium-high heat, stirring often, 8 to 10 minutes or until browned. Add onion and garlic, and sauté 5 minutes.

3. Stir in kidney beans and next 3 ingredients, and bring to a boil. Sprinkle with reserved 2 Tbsp. flour mixture, and stir until blended. Cover, reduce heat to low, and cook, stirring occasionally, 30 minutes.

smoky chicken chili

makes 9 cups · hands-on time 15 min. · total time 1 hour, 30 min.

souper tip

Save time by making this chicken chili with smoked chicken from your favorite barbecue restaurant, or use a barbecue-flavored rotisserie chicken from your supermarket.

- 2 poblano chile peppers, chopped
- 1 large red bell pepper, chopped
- 1 medium-size sweet onion, chopped
- 3 garlic cloves, minced
- 2 Tbsp. olive oil
- 2 (14½-oz.) cans zesty chili-style diced tomatoes
- 3 cups shredded or chopped smoked chicken (about 1 lb.)
- 1 (16-oz.) can navy beans
- 1 (15-oz.) can black beans, drained and rinsed
- 1 (12-oz.) can beer*
- 1 (1.25-oz.) envelope white chicken chili seasoning mix

Toppings: shredded Cheddar cheese, chopped fresh cilantro, sour cream, lime wedges, baby corn, sliced black olives, chopped red onion, tortilla chips

1. Sauté first 4 ingredients in hot oil in a large Dutch oven over medium-high heat 8 minutes or until vegetables are tender. Stir in diced tomatoes and next 5 ingredients. Bring to a boil over medium-high heat. Reduce heat to low, and simmer, stirring occasionally, 1 hour. Serve with desired toppings.

* 1½ cups low-sodium chicken broth may be substituted.

Note: We tested with Del Monte Diced Tomatoes Zesty Chili Style and McCormick White Chicken Chili Seasoning Mix.

peppers dictionary

Chile peppers are certainly known for their heat, but flavors can vary from mild to off the charts.

Feel free to mix and match and substitute chiles in the recipes to increase or decrease the heat, based on how much spice your tastebuds can handle.

Poblano
These summer peppers have rich, zesty flavor. Their dried state is called ancho.

Anaheim
Anaheims are slightly sweet chiles with mild heat. They are often stuffed.

Jalapeño
Popular peppers known for their fiery hot seeds and veins. Chipotles are the smoked, dried form.

Cubanelle
Enjoy these sweet peppers raw on a salad, or in any way you'd use a bell pepper.

Hot cherry
Also called Hungarian cherry peppers, these peppers are small, slightly rounded, and bright red. They pack a medium punch.

Serrano
Serranos are green, small, and spicy.

Sweet mini
These are miniature versions of bell peppers. Use them interchangeably.

Yellow caribe
Hot yellow peppers, caribe chiles carry a sweetly spicy, intense flavor.

Hungarian wax
These pale yellow chiles are medium-hot.

Red Fresno
Comparable in spiciness to jalapeños, red Fresno chiles are short and cone shaped. Use them sparingly, because their assertive flavor will surprise you.

Thai chiles
Also known as bird chiles, these intensely hot chiles are graded hotter than jalapeños.

Shishito
Only about two inches in length, Japanese shishito chiles are sweet and mild.

white lightning chicken chili with avocado-mango salsa

makes 11½ cups · hands-on time 25 min. · total time 30 min.

CHILI
1 large sweet onion, diced
2 garlic cloves, minced
2 Tbsp. olive oil
4 cups shredded cooked chicken
2 (14½-oz.) cans chicken broth
2 (4.5-oz.) cans chopped green chiles
1 (1.25-oz.) package white chicken chili seasoning mix
3 (16-oz.) cans navy beans, undrained

SALSA
1 large avocado, chopped
1 cup diced fresh mango
⅓ cup diced red onion
2 Tbsp. chopped fresh cilantro
2 Tbsp. fresh lime juice
Toppings: sour cream, shredded Monterey Jack cheese, fresh cilantro leaves

1. Prepare the Chili: Sauté onion and garlic in hot oil in a large Dutch oven over medium-high heat 5 minutes or until onion is tender. Stir in chicken, next 3 ingredients, and 2 cans navy beans. Coarsely mash remaining can navy beans, and stir into chicken mixture. Bring to a boil, stirring often; cover, reduce heat to medium-low, and simmer, stirring occasionally, 10 minutes.

2. Prepare the Salsa: Stir together avocado and next 4 ingredients. Serve chili with salsa and desired toppings.

Note: We tested with McCormick White Chicken Chili Seasoning Mix.

chicken-and-three bean chili verde

makes 12 cups · hands-on time 30 min. · total time 45 min.

14 fresh tomatillos (about 3 lb.), husks removed
3 garlic cloves, minced
1 extra-large chicken bouillon cube
1 large onion, chopped
3 poblano peppers, seeded and chopped
2 Tbsp. olive oil
1 (16-oz.) package frozen whole kernel white corn
1 Tbsp. chili powder
1 tsp. ground cumin
3 cups chopped cooked chicken
1 (15-oz.) can black beans, drained and rinsed
1 (15-oz.) can navy beans, drained and rinsed
1 (15-oz.) can small kidney beans, drained and rinsed
2 cups crushed tortilla chips
½ cup fresh cilantro leaves, chopped
3 Tbsp. fresh lime juice
2 tsp. table salt
½ tsp. black pepper
Toppings: avocado slices, shredded Jack cheese, fresh cilantro leaves

1. Bring first 3 ingredients and 3 cups water to a boil in a 3-qt. saucepan; boil 10 minutes.

2. Meanwhile, sauté onion and peppers in hot oil in a large Dutch oven over medium-high heat 4 minutes or until tender. Add corn; sauté 2 minutes. Add chili powder and cumin; sauté 4 minutes.

3. Remove tomatillo mixture from heat, and cool 5 minutes. Process mixture in a blender until smooth.

4. Add chicken, beans, and tomatillo mixture to Dutch oven. Cook, stirring occasionally, 15 minutes. Stir in tortilla chips and next 4 ingredients; cook 5 minutes or until tortilla chips are soft. Serve with desired toppings.

Note: We tested with Knorr Extra Large Chicken Bouillon Cubes.

tex-mex chicken chili with lime

makes 3 qt. · hands-on time 15 min. · total time 45 min.

Store-bought rotisserie chicken helps speed prep time, while white ale adds plenty of spice, body, and flavor.

1   Tbsp. butter
2   Tbsp. olive oil
1   large white onion, diced
1   medium-size red onion, diced
1   poblano or bell pepper, seeded and diced
1   red or green jalapeño pepper, seeded and diced
1   large sweet potato, peeled and chopped
2   tsp. ground cumin
2   tsp. chipotle powder
2   tsp. kosher salt
3   garlic cloves, minced
2   (16-oz.) cans navy beans, drained and rinsed
1   (12-oz.) bottle white ale
4   cups shredded deli-roasted chicken
4   cups chicken broth
Toppings: sour cream, fresh cilantro leaves, sliced green onions, lime wedges

1. Melt butter with oil in a Dutch oven over medium heat. Add white onion and next 7 ingredients, and sauté 8 minutes or until translucent. Add garlic, and cook 30 seconds.

2. Stir in beans and beer, and cook 5 minutes or until liquid is reduced by half. Add chicken and broth; bring to a boil over high heat. Reduce heat to medium-low, and simmer 30 minutes until thickened. Serve with desired toppings.

Note: We tested with Blue Moon Belgian White Belgian-Style Wheat Ale.

turkey chili

makes 4 to 6 servings · hands-on time 20 min. · total time 6 hours, 20 min.

1¼ lb. lean ground turkey
1 large onion, chopped
1 garlic clove, minced
1 (1.25-oz.) envelope chili seasoning mix
1 (12-oz.) can beer
1½ cups frozen corn kernels
1 red bell pepper, chopped
1 green bell pepper, chopped

1 (28-oz.) can crushed tomatoes
1 (15-oz.) can black beans, drained and rinsed
1 (8-oz.) can tomato sauce
¾ tsp. table salt
Toppings: shredded Cheddar cheese, finely chopped red onion, fresh jalapeño slices

souper tip

This chili recipe is as easy as it is delicious. Browning the ground turkey, onions, and garlic along with the seasoning mix and beer before adding them to the slow cooker gives this chili a richer flavor.

1. Cook first 4 ingredients in a large skillet over medium-high heat, stirring often, 8 minutes or until turkey crumbles and is no longer pink. Stir in beer; cook 2 minutes, stirring occasionally. Spoon mixture into a 5½-qt. slow cooker; stir in corn and next 6 ingredients until well blended. Cover and cook on LOW 6 hours. Serve with desired toppings.

quick turkey chili

makes 6 to 8 servings · hands-on time 10 min. · total time 56 min.

....

1	medium onion, chopped
1	Tbsp. vegetable oil
2	garlic cloves, chopped
1	lb. ground turkey
2	Tbsp. chili powder
2	tsp. ground cumin
3	Tbsp. tomato paste
1	(28-oz.) can diced tomatoes

1	(16-oz.) can red kidney beans, drained and rinsed
1	cup chicken broth
1	cup beer*
1	tsp. table salt
½	tsp. pepper
¼	cup chopped fresh cilantro
Garnish: sour cream	

1. Sauté chopped onion in hot oil in a large Dutch oven over medium-high heat 5 minutes or until tender; add garlic, and sauté 1 minute.

2. Add turkey, chili powder, and cumin, and cook, stirring often, 8 minutes or until meat crumbles and is no longer pink. Stir in tomato paste, and cook 2 minutes. Add tomatoes and next 5 ingredients. Bring mixture to a boil; cover, reduce heat to low, and simmer, stirring occasionally, 30 minutes. Stir in cilantro.

* Chicken broth may be substituted.

black bean chili

makes 8 servings · hands-on time 10 min. · total time 30 min.

If you'd like a meatier version, substitute 1 lb. of ground round for the meatless burger crumbles. Omit the vegetable oil, and sauté the meat with the onion for 10 minutes or until the meat is no longer pink, and then proceed with the recipe as directed.

3 (15-oz.) cans black beans
1 large sweet onion, chopped
1 (12-oz.) package meatless burger crumbles
2 Tbsp. vegetable oil
4 tsp. chili powder
1 tsp. ground cumin
½ tsp. pepper
¼ tsp. table salt
1 (14-oz.) can reduced-sodium fat-free chicken broth

2 (14.5-oz.) cans petite diced tomatoes with jalapeños
Toppings: sour cream, shredded Cheddar cheese, lime wedges, jalapeño peppers slices, chopped fresh cilantro, chopped tomatoes, corn chips

1. Drain and rinse 2 cans black beans. (Do not drain third can.)

2. Sauté chopped onion and burger crumbles in hot oil in a large Dutch oven over medium heat 6 minutes. Stir in chili powder and next 3 ingredients; sauté 1 minute. Stir in drained and undrained beans, chicken broth, and diced tomatoes. Bring to a boil over medium-high heat; cover, reduce heat to low, and simmer 10 minutes. Serve chili with desired toppings.

Note: We tested with Boca Meatless Ground Burger for meatless burger crumbles.

veggie chili

makes 6 cups · hands-on time 20 min. · total time 30 min.

souper tip

To chop zucchini and yellow squash for this chili, first cut the zucchini lengthwise into slices. Stack the slices, and cut lengthwise again into strips. Then, keeping the strips piled together, cut crosswise into pieces.

1	large zucchini, chopped
1	large yellow squash, chopped
1	large onion, chopped
2	Tbsp. olive oil
½	tsp. table salt
1	(12-oz.) package meatless burger crumbles
1	(25-oz.) jar Texas chili starter with red bean and Bock beer

Toppings: shredded Cheddar cheese, sour cream, sliced green onion

1. Sauté zucchini, squash, and onion in hot oil in a large Dutch oven over medium-high heat 3 to 4 minutes or until tender.

2. Add salt and crumbles; cook 1 minute. Stir in chili starter. Bring to a boil over medium-high heat; reduce heat to medium-low, and simmer, stirring occasionally, 10 minutes.

Note: We tested with Frontera All Natural Texas Chili Starter with Red Bean and Bock Beer.

four-bean veggie chili

makes 22½ cups · hands-on time 33 min. · total time 8 hours, 33 min.

Add a dash of hot sauce to your bowl if you like a little extra heat. And feel free to substitute any mix of beans that you like.

souper tip

Cool leftovers, and freeze in plastic freezer containers or zip-top plastic freezer bags for up to two months.

- 2 large carrots, diced (1 cup)
- 2 celery ribs, diced (½ cup)
- 1 medium-size sweet onion, diced
- Vegetable cooking spray
- 2 (8-oz.) packages sliced fresh mushrooms
- 1 large zucchini, chopped (1½ cups)
- 1 yellow squash, chopped (1 cup)
- 1 Tbsp. chili powder
- 1 tsp. dried basil
- 1 tsp. seasoned pepper
- 1 (8-oz.) can tomato sauce
- 3 cups tomato juice
- 2 (14½-oz.) cans diced tomatoes, undrained
- 1 (15-oz.) can pinto beans, drained and rinsed
- 1 (15-oz.) can black beans, drained and rinsed
- 1 (15-oz.) can great Northern, beans, drained and rinsed
- 1 (15-oz.) can kidney beans, drained and rinsed
- 1 cup frozen whole kernel corn

1. Sauté first 3 ingredients in a large nonstick skillet coated with cooking spray over medium-high heat 10 minutes or until onions are translucent. Add mushrooms, zucchini, and squash; sauté 3 more minutes. Add chili powder, dried basil, and seasoned pepper, and sauté 5 more minutes.

2. Stir together tomato sauce and tomato juice in a 6-qt. slow cooker until smooth. Stir in carrot mixture, diced tomatoes, and remaining ingredients. Cover and cook on LOW 8 hours.

big-batch veggie chili

makes 12 to 15 servings · hands-on time 25 min. · total time 55 min.

2 large carrots, diced
1 medium onion, diced
1 Tbsp. vegetable oil
1 (3.625-oz.) package chili seasoning kit
1 (8-oz.) can tomato sauce
3 cups tomato juice
2 (14.5-oz.) cans diced tomatoes, undrained
2 (15-oz.) cans black beans, drained and rinsed
2 (15-oz.) cans great Northern beans, drained and rinsed
1 large zucchini, chopped
1 yellow squash, chopped
1 cup frozen whole kernel corn

Toppings: chopped fresh cilantro, sour cream, chopped green onions, shredded sharp Cheddar cheese, chopped tomatoes

1. Sauté carrots and onion in hot oil in a 5- to 6-qt. Dutch oven over medium heat 7 minutes or until onions are translucent. Stir in half of red pepper packet from chili kit; stir in all of remaining packets. Sauté mixture 2 minutes. Stir in tomato sauce and next 7 ingredients.

2. Bring to a boil; cover, reduce heat to medium low, and simmer, stirring occasionally, 30 minutes or until vegetables are tender. Serve with desired toppings.

Note: We tested with Wick Fowler's 2-Alarm Chili Kit.

Curried Chicken
Chowder, page 162

gumbos stews and chowders

shrimp-and-sausage gumbo

makes 6 servings · hands-on time 27 min. · total time 5 hours, 57 min.

½ cup all-purpose flour
1 lb. andouille sausage, sliced
1 (14.5-oz.) can diced tomatoes
1 large onion, chopped
1 large green bell pepper, chopped
2 celery ribs, chopped
4 garlic cloves, chopped
3 bay leaves

2 tsp. Creole seasoning
½ tsp. dried thyme
4 cups chicken broth
3 lb. unpeeled, large raw shrimp, peeled and deveined
1 bunch green onions, sliced
¼ cup chopped fresh flat-leaf parsley
Garnish: sliced green onions

souper tip

Serve with an easy-to-make herbed rice: Stir together 3 cups hot cooked rice and ¼ cup chopped fresh flat-leaf parsley for additional color and flavor.

1. Preheat oven to 400°. Sprinkle flour in a 9-inch cast-iron skillet. Bake 10 to 15 minutes or until golden brown, stirring once. Cool 10 minutes.

2. Meanwhile, cook sausage in a Dutch oven over medium heat, stirring occasionally, 5 minutes or until browned. Drain on paper towels. Place sausage in a 6-qt. slow cooker; add tomatoes and next 7 ingredients.

3. Whisk together browned flour and broth until smooth. Pour into slow cooker. Cover and cook on HIGH 5 to 6 hours. Stir in shrimp, green onions, and parsley. Cover and cook on HIGH 30 minutes, stirring once. Discard bay leaves before serving.

chicken-andouille gumbo with roasted potatoes

makes 10 cups · hands-on time 53 min. · total time 2 hours, 23 min.

souper tip

Try a chicken-and-shrimp twist: Prepare recipe through Step 3. Stir in ½ to ¾ lb. peeled and deveined, medium-size raw shrimp (31/40 count). Cook 5 minutes or just until shrimp turn pink.

1 lb. andouille sausage, cut into ¼-inch-thick slices
½ cup peanut oil
¾ cup all-purpose flour
1 large onion, coarsely chopped
1 red bell pepper, coarsely chopped
1 cup thinly sliced celery
2 garlic cloves, minced
2 tsp. Cajun seasoning
⅛ tsp. ground red pepper (optional)
1 (48-oz.) container chicken broth
2 lb. skinned and boned chicken breasts
Roasted Potatoes
Toppings: chopped fresh parsley, cooked and crumbled bacon, hot sauce

1. Cook sausage in a large skillet over medium heat, stirring often, 7 minutes or until browned. Remove sausage; drain and pat dry with paper towels.

2. Heat oil in a stainless-steel Dutch oven over medium heat; gradually whisk in flour, and cook, whisking constantly, 18 to 20 minutes or until flour is caramel-colored. (Do not burn mixture.) Reduce heat to low, and cook, whisking constantly, until mixture is milk chocolate-colored and texture is smooth (about 2 minutes).

3. Increase heat to medium. Stir in onion, next 4 ingredients, and, if desired, ground red pepper. Cook, stirring constantly, 3 minutes. Gradually stir in chicken broth; add chicken and sausage. Increase heat to medium-high, and bring to a boil. Reduce heat to low, and simmer, stirring occasionally, 1 hour and 30 minutes to 1 hour and 40 minutes or until chicken is done. Shred chicken into large pieces using 2 forks.

4. Place Roasted Potatoes in serving bowls. Spoon gumbo over potatoes. Serve immediately with desired toppings.

roasted potatoes

makes 6 to 8 servings · hands-on time 5 min. · total time 45 min.

3   lb. baby red potatoes,
    quartered

1   Tbsp. peanut oil
1   tsp. kosher salt

1. Preheat oven to 450°. Stir together all ingredients in a large bowl. Place potatoes in a single layer in a lightly greased 15- x 10-inch jelly-roll pan. Bake 40 to 45 minutes or until tender and browned, stirring twice.

mastering roux

Roux provides a rich foundation of flavor for gumbo. Follow these tips for the best results.

To make roux (pronounced "roo"), you simply combine fat and flour in a heavy skillet (cast iron is a favorite) or pot and cook it, stirring constantly, until the raw flavor of the flour cooks out and the roux has achieved the desired color—blonde to dark brown. This process coaxes out maximum flavor and a properly cooked roux gives body and adds nutty flavor while thickening soups, stews, and sauces. One simple roux commandment to live by: Pay attention. No texting and stirring at the same time.

1

2

3

Pick your fat. Butter or animal fat adds flavor, but use canola oil for darker Creole and Cajun roux. Its higher smoke point is more forgiving.

Choose your heat. Heat fat in a pan over medium heat. Add roughly a 1:1 ratio of flour to fat. Gradually whisk in the flour to form a thick paste. The roux will thin out and become smooth as it cooks.

Keep stirring until your roux reaches the desired color. Frequent stirring keeps the roux from clumping and burning.

1. BLONDE ROUX: Flour is cooked but still light. Stir into sauces such as velouté to add richness and body.

2. LIGHT BROWN ROUX: Marry this versatile thickener with pan juices from a roast to make gravy.

3. MEDIUM-BROWN ROUX: Begins losing thickening power but adds toasty flavor. Takes 15 minutes on medium heat.

4. DARK BROWN ROUX: Takes 20 minutes when cooked fast, up to 1 hour cooked slowly. Gives those étouffées and gumbos deep, smoky flavor.

5. BLESS YOUR HEART: You've gone too far. Cook the roux too long or fast, and it will taste burned.

gumbo z'herbes

makes 10 to 12 servings · hands-on time 55 min. · total time 2 hours, 50 min.

souper tip

Green gumbo or gumbo z'herbes is traditionally made during lent on Maundy Thursday and served on Good Friday. Gumbo z'herbes includes many different kinds of greens—and you should always include an odd number of the green leafy ingredients. The saying goes that for every different green you add, you will find a new friend in the coming year.

5 cups chopped mustard greens
5 cups chopped collard greens
5 cups chopped turnip greens
3 cups chopped beet tops (5 oz.)
2 cups chopped cabbage
2 cups chopped romaine lettuce
2 cups chopped watercress
1½ cups coarsely chopped spinach
1 cup chopped carrot tops (1½ oz.)

2 garlic cloves, chopped
1 medium onion, chopped
½ lb. smoked sausage, diced
½ lb. smoked ham, diced
½ lb. uncooked beef brisket, diced
½ lb. dry Spanish chorizo or andouille sausage, diced
3 Tbsp. vegetable oil
¼ cup all-purpose flour
2 tsp. table salt
½ tsp. fresh thyme leaves
½ tsp. ground red pepper
½ tsp. filé powder
Hot cooked rice

1. Combine first 11 ingredients and water to cover in a 15-qt. stockpot; cover. Bring to a boil over high heat (about 20 minutes). Uncover; boil, stirring occasionally, 30 minutes. Drain, reserving cooking liquid. Coarsely chop greens.

2. Combine smoked sausage and next 2 ingredients in pot with 2 cups reserved cooking liquid. Bring to a boil, stirring once, 15 minutes.

3. Meanwhile, cook chorizo in hot oil in a medium skillet over medium-low heat, stirring occasionally, 10 minutes or until browned. Remove with a slotted spoon; drain on paper towels, reserving 3 Tbsp. drippings in skillet.

4. Make a roux: Stir flour into reserved drippings with a wooden spoon, and cook over medium heat, stirring constantly, until flour is medium brown (about 15 minutes). Add flour mixture to mixture in stockpot, and stir well. Add chopped greens mixture and 5 cups reserved cooking liquid. Reduce heat to medium-low; simmer, stirring occasionally, 20 minutes. Stir in salt, thyme, red pepper, and chorizo. Cook, stirring occasionally, 40 minutes. Stir in filé powder; stir vigorously. Serve over hot cooked rice.

spiced beef stew with sweet potatoes

makes 8 servings · hands-on time 50 min. · total time 6 hours, 50 min.

Serve this hearty main-dish stew with Green Chile Biscuits (page 200).

1 (6-oz.) can tomato paste
1 (32-oz.) container beef broth
1 (3-lb.) boneless chuck roast, trimmed and cut into 1½-inch cubes
3 Tbsp. all-purpose flour
1½ tsp. table salt
1 tsp. freshly ground pepper
2 Tbsp. olive oil
2 lb. small sweet potatoes, peeled and cubed

2 sweet onions, cut into eighths
2 cups cubed butternut squash (about 1 lb.)
2 cups frozen whole kernel corn, thawed
2 celery ribs, sliced
4 garlic cloves, minced
2 tsp. ancho chile powder
1 tsp. smoked paprika
1 tsp. dried thyme

1. Whisk together first 2 ingredients until smooth.

2. Sprinkle beef with flour, salt, and pepper; toss to coat.

3. Cook beef, in batches, in hot oil in a large skillet over medium-high heat, stirring occasionally, 10 to 12 minutes or until browned. Place in a 6-qt. slow cooker. Add sweet potatoes, next 8 ingredients, and broth mixture. Cover and cook on HIGH 6 to 7 hours or until tender.

red wine beef stew

makes 6 to 8 servings · hands-on time 20 min. · total time 3 hours, 26 min.

souper tip

Deglazing the Dutch oven—stirring in the wine to loosen the browned bits from the bottom—adds rich flavor to the sauce for this dish. These bits are small pieces of meat that have stuck to the pan and the caramel-ized drippings from the juices of the meat.

1 (4-lb.) boneless chuck roast, trimmed
4 Tbsp. all-purpose flour, divided
1¾ tsp. table salt, divided
1 tsp. paprika
½ tsp. pepper
2 Tbsp. vegetable oil
1 cup dry red wine*
2 (14½-oz.) cans low-sodium beef broth
½ tsp. dried thyme
1 bay leaf
1 small turnip
1 (8-oz.) package fresh mushrooms
1 (16-oz.) package baby carrots
Garnish: thinly sliced fresh chives

1. Cut beef into 2- to 2½-inch pieces; pat with paper towels to absorb excess moisture. Combine 3 Tbsp. flour, 1 tsp. salt, paprika, and pepper in a bowl; toss beef with flour mixture.

2. Cook beef, in batches, in hot oil in a Dutch oven over medium-high heat, stirring often, 4 to 6 minutes or until brown. Remove beef from Dutch oven. Add red wine, stirring to loosen particles from bottom of Dutch oven. Return beef to Dutch oven; add broth, thyme, bay leaf, and ½ tsp. salt. Bring to a boil. Cover, reduce heat to low, and cook, stirring occasionally, 1 hour.

3. Meanwhile, peel turnip, and cut into 1-inch cubes. Halve mushrooms. Add turnip, mushrooms, and carrots to stew. Cover and cook, stirring occasionally, 1 to 1½ hours or until meat is fork-tender.

4. Whisk together remaining 1 Tbsp. flour and ¼ tsp. salt until blended; whisk ½ cup hot broth into flour mixture until smooth. Whisk flour mixture into stew until smooth. Cook, stirring often, 20 minutes or until thickened.

* Beef broth may be substituted.

rosemary lamb stew

makes 4 servings · hands-on time 30 min. · total time 1 hour

Onions, carrots, and garlic give this easy stew its foundation of flavor, and stewed tomatoes make it saucy. Serve it over hot cooked rice.

1   cup chopped yellow onion
1   Tbsp. olive oil
1   (8-oz.) package sliced fresh mushrooms
1   cup sliced carrots
2½ cups diced cooked lamb
2   garlic cloves, minced
1   (14½-oz.) can stewed tomatoes
½   cup chicken broth
1   fresh rosemary sprig
1   tsp. kosher salt
½   tsp. freshly ground black pepper
Hot cooked rice
Garnish: fresh rosemary sprig

1. Sauté onion in hot oil in a 3-qt. saucepan over medium-high heat 3 to 4 minutes or until tender. Add mushrooms and carrots, and cook, stirring occasionally, 5 minutes. Add lamb and garlic, and cook, stirring constantly, 3 minutes. Stir in tomatoes, broth, and rosemary. Bring to a boil; reduce heat to medium-low, and simmer, stirring occasionally, 30 minutes. Stir in salt and pepper. Discard rosemary sprig. Serve stew over hot cooked rice.

mexican pork stew

makes about 11 cups · hands-on time 25 min. · total time 1 hour, 56 min.

6   green onions, trimmed
1   bunch cilantro
Kitchen string
2½ lb. boneless pork shoulder
     roast
1   tsp. table salt
1   tsp. pepper
3   garlic cloves
1   (10-oz.) can mild red
     enchilada sauce
2   medium-size baking
     potatoes, peeled and
     diced

10   (5½-inch) soft taco-size
     corn tortillas
2   (11-oz.) cans yellow corn
     with red and green bell
     peppers
Salt to taste
**Toppings: lemon wedges,
     sliced radishes, diced
     onion, shredded cabbage**

1. Tie green onions and cilantro together with kitchen string. Trim and discard fat from pork, and cut pork into ¼-inch pieces. Season with salt and pepper.

2. Cook pork, in 3 batches, in a large Dutch oven over medium-high heat 5 to 7 minutes or until browned. Bring pork, garlic, and 6 cups water to a boil; skim fat, and discard. Cover, reduce heat to low, and simmer 30 minutes or until meat is tender. Stir in onion-and-cilantro bundle, enchilada sauce, and potatoes. Bring to a boil over medium-high heat; reduce heat to low, and simmer 20 minutes or just until potatoes are tender.

3. Meanwhile, heat tortillas, 1 at a time, in a hot nonstick skillet over medium-high heat 20 to 30 seconds on each side. Wrap tortillas in a towel to keep warm.

4. Remove and discard onion-and-cilantro bundle. Increase heat to medium. Stir in corn, and cook, uncovered, stirring occasionally, 8 to 10 minutes or until thoroughly heated. Season with salt to taste.

5. Serve soup with desired toppings and warm tortillas.

brunswick stew

makes 8 servings · hands-on time 15 min. · total time 12 hours, 15 min.

This hearty Southern stew has a slightly sweet flavor thanks to the barbecue sauce, although some variations use chili sauce or ketchup.

3 lb. boneless pork shoulder roast (Boston Butt)

3 medium-size new potatoes, peeled and chopped

1 large onion, chopped

1 (28-oz.) can crushed tomatoes

1 (18-oz.) bottle barbecue sauce

1 (14-oz.) can chicken broth

1 (9-oz.) package frozen baby lima beans, thawed

1 (9-oz.) package frozen corn, thawed

6 Tbsp. brown sugar

1 tsp. table salt

souper tip

Low, slow cooking for a long time makes the pork extremely tender, so it shreds easily. High heat will yield less tender results.

1. Trim roast, and cut into 2-inch pieces. Stir together all ingredients in a 6-qt. slow cooker.

2. Cover and cook on LOW 10 to 12 hours or until potatoes are fork-tender. Remove pork with a slotted spoon, and shred. Return shredded pork to slow cooker, and stir well. Ladle stew into bowls.

summer brunswick stew

makes 10 servings · hands-on tme 28 min. · total time 58 min.

A light, summery broth lets the flavors of fresh-picked corn and lady peas shine. Stir in whatever barbecue sauce you have on hand—some are bolder or sweeter than others, so start with the minimum amount and adjust according to taste.

1	large sweet onion, diced	1	lb. Yukon gold potatoes, peeled and diced (about 2 cups)
2	Tbsp. olive oil		
2	garlic cloves, minced		
6	cups chicken broth	2	cups fresh corn kernels (about 4 ears)
2	cups fresh lady peas or butter peas	1	to 1½ cups barbecue sauce
1	lb. pulled barbecued pork (without sauce)	2	cups peeled and diced tomatoes

1. Sauté onion in hot oil in a Dutch oven over medium heat 5 minutes or until tender; add garlic, and sauté 1 minute. Add broth and peas; bring to a boil, stirring often. Cover, reduce heat to medium-low, and simmer, stirring occasionally, 15 minutes or until peas are tender. Stir in pork and next 3 ingredients; cover and simmer, stirring occasionally, 15 minutes or until potatoes are tender. Add tomatoes, and season with salt and pepper to taste.

Note: We tested with Kraft Original Barbecue Sauce.

souper tip

Georgia says Brunswick stew, while Kentucky claims it's called burgoo. Regardless of the name, the two stews are almost identical. While both Georgia and Virginia lay claim as the birthplace of Brunswick stew, the origin is yet to be declared. In Kentucky, a large camp-style pot of meat, vegetables, and seasonings is cooked up practically the same way as Brunswick stew and with the same ingredients. The main difference is that burgoo usually contains mutton, as well as other meats.

chicken-and-brisket brunswick stew

makes 16 cups · hands-on time 25 min. · total time 2 hours, 40 min.

2 large onions, chopped
2 garlic cloves, minced
1 Tbsp. vegetable oil
1½ Tbsp. jarred beef soup base
2 lb. skinned and boned chicken breasts
1 (28-oz.) can fire-roasted crushed tomatoes
1 (12-oz.) package frozen white shoepeg or whole kernel corn
1 (10-oz.) package frozen cream-style corn, thawed

1 (9-oz.) package frozen baby lima beans
1 (12-oz.) bottle chili sauce
1 Tbsp. brown sugar
1 Tbsp. yellow mustard
1 Tbsp. Worcestershire sauce
½ tsp. coarsely ground pepper
1 lb. chopped barbecued beef brisket (without sauce)
1 Tbsp. fresh lemon juice
Hot sauce (optional)

1. Sauté onions and garlic in hot oil in a 7.5-qt. Dutch oven over medium-high heat 3 to 5 minutes or until tender.

2. Stir together beef soup base and 2 cups water, and add to Dutch oven. Stir in chicken and next 9 ingredients. Bring to a boil. Cover, reduce heat to low, and cook, stirring occasionally, 2 hours.

3. Uncover and shred chicken into large pieces using 2 forks. Stir in brisket and lemon juice. Cover and cook 10 minutes. Serve with hot sauce, if desired.

Note: We tested with Superior Touch Better Than Bouillon Beef Base and Muir Glen Organic Fire Roasted Crushed Tomatoes.

kentucky burgoo

makes 15 servings · hands-on time 23 min. · total time 1 hour, 43 min.

- 2 (6-oz.) skinless bone-in chicken breast halves
- ¾ lb. boneless pork loin roast trimmed
- 1 tsp. olive oil
- Vegetable cooking spray
- 2 cups chopped onion (about 1 large)
- 1¾ cups sliced carrot
- 1½ cups chopped celery
- 1 cup chopped green bell pepper
- 3 garlic cloves, minced
- 2 (14½-oz.) cans diced tomatoes with basil, garlic, and oregano
- 1½ cups packaged angel hair coleslaw
- 1 tsp. dried thyme
- ½ tsp. table salt
- ½ tsp. black pepper
- ¼ tsp. ground red pepper
- 1 (16-oz.) package frozen vegetable soup mix with tomatoes
- 2 (14½-oz.) cans reduced-sodium fat-free chicken broth
- 1 (14½-oz.) can beef broth
- 2 (5.5-oz.) cans spicy-hot vegetable juice
- ⅓ cup chopped fresh parsley

1. Preheat oven to 375°. Arrange chicken and pork roast on a lightly greased 15- x 10-inch jelly-roll pan. Bake 35 minutes or until done. Remove chicken and pork roast from pan; cool. Shred meat with 2 forks.

2. Heat oil over medium-high heat in a large Dutch oven coated with cooking spray. Add onion and next 4 ingredients; sauté 8 minutes or until tender. Stir in shredded meat, tomato, and next 9 ingredients. Bring to a boil; cover, reduce heat, and simmer 45 minutes. Stir in parsley.

Note: We tested with McKenzie's Frozen Vegetable Soup Mix with Tomatoes and V-8 Spicy-Hot Vegetable Juice.

chicken sausage-and-white bean stew

makes 4 servings · hands-on time 16 min. · total time 8 hours, 11 min.

1 (12-oz.) package spinach and feta chicken sausage, sliced
3 carrots, coarsely chopped
1 medium onion, chopped
½ tsp. table salt
½ tsp. chopped fresh rosemary
¼ tsp. pepper

1 (14½-oz.) can fire-roasted diced tomatoes
2 (15.8-oz.) cans great Northern beans, drained and rinsed
1 (5-oz.) bag fresh spinach
4 bacon slices, cooked and crumbled

1. Cook sausage in a large skillet over medium-high heat 4 minutes or until browned.

2. Place carrot and onion in a 4- or 5-qt. slow cooker; sprinkle with salt, rosemary, and pepper. Layer tomatoes and beans over carrot mixture. Top with sausage. Cover and cook on LOW 8 hours or until vegetables are tender. Stir in spinach; cook 10 minutes. Sprinkle with bacon before serving.

40-minute chicken and dumplings

makes 4 to 6 servings · hands-on time 30 min. · total time 40 min.

souper tip

Don't cook more dumplings at once than will lie in a single layer on top of the broth. If overcrowded, they'll get soggy and break apart. Keep broth at a gentle simmer. Boiling will tear the dumplings apart.

Convenience products like deli-roasted chicken, cream of chicken soup, and canned biscuits make a quick-and-tasty version of classic chicken and dumplings.

1 (32-oz.) container low-sodium chicken broth
3 cups shredded cooked chicken (about 1½ lb.)
1 (10¾-oz.) can reduced-fat cream of chicken soup
¼ tsp. poultry seasoning
1 (10.2-oz.) can refrigerated jumbo buttermilk biscuits
2 carrots, diced
3 celery ribs, diced

1. Bring first 4 ingredients to a boil in a Dutch oven over medium-high heat. Cover, reduce heat to low, and simmer, stirring occasionally, 5 minutes. Increase heat to medium-high; return to a low boil.

2. Place biscuits on a lightly floured surface. Roll or pat each biscuit to ⅛-inch thickness; cut into ½-inch-wide strips.

3. Drop strips, 1 at a time, into simmering broth mixture. Add carrots and celery. Cover, reduce heat to low, and simmer 15 to 20 minutes, stirring occasionally to prevent dumplings from sticking.

Note: One roasted chicken yields about 3 cups of meat.

chicken and cornbread dumplings

makes 8 servings · hands-on time 30 min. · total time 5 hours, 40 min.

Chicken

3 skinned, bone-in chicken breasts (about 1½ lb.)

6 skinned and boned chicken thighs (about 1 lb.)

1 tsp. table salt

½ tsp. freshly ground pepper

½ tsp. poultry seasoning

½ lb. carrots, sliced

½ lb. parsnips, sliced

4 celery ribs, sliced

1 sweet onion, chopped

2 (10¾-oz.) cans cream of chicken soup

1 (32-oz.) container chicken broth

Cornbread Dumplings

1½ cups all-purpose flour

½ cup self-rising yellow cornmeal

2 tsp. baking powder

½ tsp. table salt

1 cup milk

3 Tbsp. butter, melted

¼ tsp. dried thyme

2 tsp. chopped fresh flat-leaf parsley

Garnish: fresh parsley leaves

souper tip

For the best results, it is a good idea to test baking powder before using it in a recipe. Stir together a little bit of warm water and baking powder. If you see bubbles form, then you're good to go. If no bubbles form, it's time to replace your baking powder.

1. Prepare Chicken: Rub chicken pieces with salt, pepper, and poultry seasoning. Place breasts in a 6-qt. slow cooker; top with thighs. Add carrot and next 3 ingredients. Whisk together soup and broth until smooth. Pour soup mixture over vegetables. Cover and cook on HIGH 3½ hours or until chicken shreds easily with a fork. Remove chicken; cool 10 minutes. Bone and shred chicken. Stir chicken into soup-and-vegetable mixture. Cover and cook on HIGH 1 hour or until boiling.

2. Meanwhile, prepare Cornbread Dumplings: Whisk together flour and next 3 ingredients. Make a well in center of mixture. Add milk, butter, thyme, and parsley to dry ingredients, gently stirring just until moistened.

3. Drop dough by ¼ cupfuls into simmering chicken mixture, leaving about ¼-inch space between dumplings. Cover and cook on HIGH 30 to 35 minutes or until dumplings have doubled in size.

chicken and sweet potato dumplings

makes 8 servings · hands-on time 1 hour · total time 5 hours, 50 min.

Start with a whole chicken to create a flavorful, refined broth.

1	(3¾-lb.) whole chicken
2	celery ribs, chopped
2	carrots, chopped
1	medium onion, quartered
4	garlic cloves, crushed
3	fresh thyme sprigs
1½	tsp. kosher salt
½	tsp. pepper

½	medium onion, thinly sliced
2	carrots, sliced
1	celery rib, thinly sliced
	Sweet Potato Dumplings
	Shaved Parmesan cheese
	Flat-leaf parsley leaves

1. Bring chicken, next 7 ingredients, and water to cover to a boil in a Dutch oven over medium heat. Cover, reduce heat to medium-low, and simmer 1 hour.

2. Remove chicken, reserving broth in Dutch oven. Cool chicken 30 minutes.

3. Meanwhile, cook reserved broth in Dutch oven over low heat 30 minutes.

4. Skin, bone, and shred chicken, reserving bones. Place bones in broth. Cover and chill shredded chicken until ready to use.

5. Continue cooking broth, uncovered, over low heat 1 hour or until reduced by one-third. Pour broth through a wire-mesh strainer into a bowl; discard solids. Wipe Dutch oven clean; pour broth back into Dutch oven.

6. Skim fat from broth. Add thinly sliced onion and next 2 ingredients to broth; cook over medium-high heat, stirring occasionally, 20 minutes or until carrots are crisp-tender. Add shredded chicken; return to a simmer.

7. Add Sweet Potato Dumplings to soup. Sprinkle with Parmesan and parsley. Serve immediately.

sweet potato dumplings

makes 4 dozen · hands-on time 34 min. · total time 2 hours

Sweet potatoes create flavorful, pillowy, gnocchi-like dumplings and offer a dose of vitamin C, beta-carotene, calcium, and potassium.

2 **medium-size baking potatoes (about ¾ lb.)**
1 **large sweet potato (about ½ lb.)**
¼ **cup (1 oz.) freshly grated Parmesan cheese**
1 **large egg**
½ **tsp. chopped fresh rosemary**
¼ **tsp. kosher salt**
¼ **tsp. freshly ground pepper**
½ **cup all-purpose flour**

1. Preheat oven to 400°. Prick all potatoes with a fork, and bake on a jelly-roll pan 1 hour.

2. Cool potatoes 20 minutes. Peel and mash until smooth. Add cheese and next 4 ingredients, and stir until smooth. Fold in flour just until blended.

3. Divide dough into 4 equal portions; dust with flour. Roll each into a ¾-inch-diameter rope on a well-floured surface. Cut into 1-inch pieces; place dumplings on a lightly floured baking sheet.

4. Cook dumplings, 10 to 12 at a time, in 3 qt. boiling water over medium-high heat 3 minutes. Remove with a slotted spoon.

shrimp-and-sausage stew

makes 10 to 12 servings · hands-on time 30 min. · total time 3 hours, 35 min.

· ·

4 lb. peeled, large raw shrimp
3 large onions, cut into 1-inch pieces
¼ cup vegetable oil
2 (15-oz.) cans tomato sauce
3 (14½-oz.) cans diced tomatoes with zesty green chiles
5 celery ribs, cut into 1-inch pieces
3 green bell peppers, seeded and cut into 1-inch strips

6 garlic cloves, chopped and divided
1 (1-lb.) package spicy smoked sausage, sliced
3 cups uncooked jasmine or long-grain rice
6 green onions, chopped
1 cup chopped fresh parsley
2 Tbsp. Cajun seasoning
¼ cup cornstarch
Garnish: sliced green onion

1. Butterfly shrimp by making a deep slit down back of each from large end to tail, cutting to but not through inside curve of shrimp. Devein shrimp, and store in an airtight container in the refrigerator until ready to use.

2. Cook onions in hot oil in a large Dutch oven over medium heat, stirring often, 35 to 40 minutes or until golden brown. Add tomato sauce, and cook, stirring occasionally, 25 to 30 minutes or until thickened. Add diced tomatoes with green chiles, celery, bell peppers, and 2 cups water.

3. Bring to a boil over medium-high heat; reduce heat to medium, and simmer 30 minutes or until sauce thickens slightly. Add 3 garlic cloves, and simmer 30 minutes, stirring in 1 to 2 cups of water as needed to maintain a stew-like consistency. Stir in sausage, and simmer 30 minutes, stirring in 1 to 2 cups water as needed. Skim grease from surface as needed.

4. Meanwhile, prepare rice according to package directions.

5. Stir green onions, parsley, Cajun seasoning, and remaining 3 garlic cloves into sausage mixture. Simmer 10 minutes. Add shrimp, and bring to a boil over medium-high heat.

6. Stir together cornstarch and ½ cup water. Stir into shrimp-and-sausage mixture, stirring just until mixture is thick and glossy. Serve with hot cooked rice.

soup dictionary

As you master your soup-making skills, know the difference between a broth and a stock and a chowder and a bisque.

Broth
An all-purpose, flavorful liquid that results from simmering vegetables, meat, poultry, or seafood in water.

Stock
The strained liquid from vegetables, meat, poultry, or fish that is simmered with seasonings.

Consommé
A clear broth that is enriched with meat and vegetables and clarified with egg white.

Bisque
A thick, rich soup usually consisting of pureed seafood (sometimes poultry or vegetables) and cream.

Chowder
Any thick, rich soup containing chunks of food, often either seafood or vegetables. Common examples include clam chowder and corn chowder.

Stew
A general term used to describe dishes that feature meats or vegetables that are barely covered in liquid and simmered slowly in a covered pot for a long period of time. The result is a dish with tender meats and/or vegetables in a thick soup-like broth.

Cioppino
A hearty Italian-style tomato-based stew filled with a variety of fish and shellfish.

Bouillabaisse
A seafood stew that contains a variety of fresh fish and shellfish along with onions, tomato, garlic, herbs, and white wine. It's typically served over French bread.

Cassoulet
A rustic French dish made with white beans and a variety of meats or poultry, stewed in a covered pan for a long period of time in order to develop the complex flavors.

Ragoût
A very thick, well-seasoned stew of meat, poultry, fish, or vegetables that is often served over mashed potatoes, grits, or pasta.

Gumbo
A thick soup that may contain chicken, sausage, ham, shrimp, or oysters, and often a combination of seafood and meats. It gets its flavor from a rich brown roux (mixture of flour and fat) that is cooked slowly to develop a nutty taste. Gumbo is often thickened with either okra or filé powder.

preparing homemade broth

Homemade broth is the base for many hearty soups and stews, and it's easy to prepare. Follow these tips to make your own.

1. Combine 6 lbs. chicken pieces; 2½ qts. cold water; 3 celery ribs with leaves, cut in half; 2 onions, quartered; 2 fresh thyme sprigs or ½ tsp. dried thyme; 1 bay leaf; 1½ tsp. salt; and ¾ tsp. pepper in a large Dutch oven.

2. Bring to a boil; cover, reduce heat, and simmer 1½ hours.

3. Line a large wire-mesh strainer with a double layer of cheesecloth; place in a large bowl. Pour broth through strainer, discarding chicken pieces, vegetables, and herbs. Cover broth, and chill thoroughly.

4. Skim and discard solidified fat from top of broth. This makes a large quantity: 10 cups. Store broth in a tightly covered container in the refrigerator up to 3 days, or freeze up to 3 months. Thaw and use in recipes that call for chicken broth.

gulf coast seafood stew

makes 6 to 8 servings · hands-on time 46 min. · total time 1 hour, 6 min.

1½ lb. unpeeled, medium-size raw shrimp
2 celery ribs
1 large sweet onion
2 qt. reduced-sodium fat-free chicken broth
12 oz. andouille sausage, cut into ½-inch pieces
1 poblano pepper, seeded and chopped
1 green bell pepper, chopped
1 Tbsp. canola oil
3 garlic cloves, chopped
1 lb. small red potatoes, halved
1 (12-oz.) bottle beer
1 Tbsp. fresh thyme leaves
2 fresh bay leaves
2 tsp. Creole seasoning
1½ lb. fresh white fish fillets, (such as snapper, grouper, or catfish), cubed
1 lb. cooked crawfish tails (optional)
Kosher salt and black pepper

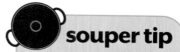

souper tip

This rustic stew was inspired by the rich, meaty flavors of a crawfish or shrimp boil. Feel free to leave the crawfish whole or sub- stitute more shrimp for the crawfish, if desired.

1. Peel shrimp; place shells in a saucepan. (Refrigerate shrimp until ready to use.) Add celery ends and onion peel to pan; chop remaining celery and onion. (Using the leftover bits of onion and celery will layer the flavor and result in a flavorful broth.) Add broth; bring to a boil over medium-high heat. Reduce heat to low; simmer 30 minutes.

2. Meanwhile, cook sausage in a large Dutch oven over medium-high heat, stirring often, 7 to 8 minutes or until browned. Remove sausage; pat dry. Wipe Dutch oven clean. Sauté celery, onion, and peppers in hot oil in Dutch oven over medium-high heat 5 to 7 minutes or until onion is tender. Add garlic, and sauté 45 seconds to 1 minute or until fragrant. Stir in pota- toes, next 4 ingredients, and sausage.

3. Pour broth mixture through a fine wire-mesh strainer into Dutch oven, dis- carding solids. Increase heat to high, and bring to a boil. Reduce heat to low, and cook, stirring occasionally, 20 to 30 minutes or until potatoes are tender.

4. Add fish; cook 2 to 3 minutes or until just opaque. Add shrimp, and cook 2 to 3 minutes or just until shrimp turn pink. If desired, stir in crawfish, and cook 2 to 3 minutes or until hot. Discard bay leaves. Add salt and pepper to taste.

5. Spoon seafood into warmed soup bowls. Top with desired amount of broth. Serve immediately.

yellow squash-and-curry stew

makes 4 servings · hands-on time 15 min. · total time 45 min.

souper tip

Roasting the squash in the oven concentrates its flavor, and curry powder gives it a sweet and fragrant kick.

2   lb. yellow squash, coarsely chopped
1   medium-size sweet onion, coarsely chopped
1   pt. grape tomatoes
3   garlic cloves, thinly sliced
2   Tbsp. olive oil
2   tsp. curry powder
¼   tsp. dried crushed red pepper

1½ tsp. kosher salt, divided
3   cups organic vegetable or chicken broth, divided
2   Tbsp. butter
1   Tbsp. fresh lime juice
½   cup torn fresh basil
¼   cup loosely packed fresh flat-leaf parsley leaves

1. Preheat oven to 450°. Toss together first 7 ingredients and 1 tsp. salt. Arrange in a single layer in a 15- x 10-inch jelly-roll pan.

2. Bake at 450° for 30 to 35 minutes or until vegetables are tender and lightly browned, stirring halfway through. Remove from oven; process 2 cups squash mixture and 1 cup broth in a blender or food processor until smooth. Divide remaining squash mixture among 4 shallow soup bowls.

3. Stir together vegetable puree and remaining 2 cups broth in a 3-qt. saucepan; bring to a boil over medium heat, stirring occasionally. Remove from heat; whisk in butter, lime juice, and remaining ½ tsp. salt.

4. Spoon broth mixture over squash mixture in bowls. Sprinkle with fresh herbs, and serve immediately.

quick shrimp chowder

makes 12 cups · hands-on time 15 min. · total time 35 min.

2   Tbsp. butter
1   medium onion, chopped
2   (10¾-oz.) cans cream of
      potato soup, undiluted
3½ cups milk
¼   tsp. ground red pepper
1½ lb. medium-size raw
      shrimp, peeled*

1   cup (4 oz.) shredded
      Monterey Jack cheese
Garnish: chopped fresh
      parsley
Oyster crackers (optional)

souper tip

We've streamlined this favorite creamy shrimp chowder by using canned soup as the base.

1. Melt butter in a Dutch oven over medium heat; add onion, and sauté 8 minutes or until tender. Stir in soup, milk, and pepper; bring to a boil. Add shrimp; reduce heat, and simmer, stirring often, 5 minutes or just until shrimp turn pink. Stir in cheese until melted. Serve immediately. Serve with oyster crackers, if desired.

* 1½ lb. frozen shrimp, thawed; 1½ lb. peeled crawfish tails; or 3 cups chopped cooked chicken may be substituted.

curried chicken chowder

makes about 16 cups · hands-on time 40 min. · total time 1 hour

souper tip

To preserve the textures of meat and vegetables in hot soup, it's important to cool the soup completely before freezing. To quickly reduce the temperature, transfer to a large, shallow container (13- x 9-inch baking dish). Refrigerate uncovered, stirring occasionally, until cool. Transfer to airtight containers or zip-top plastic freezer bags. Freeze up to one month. Thaw soup in refrigerator 8 hours.

Warm up and fill up with a big batch of Curried Chicken Chowder. The coconut milk adds a touch of sweetness to the curried soup.

2   cups diced sweet onion (about 1 large)
1   cup diced celery
1   cup diced carrots
2   Tbsp. canola oil
2   garlic cloves, minced
6   cups chicken broth
1   lb. Yukon gold potatoes, peeled and cubed
1   lb. sweet potatoes, peeled and cubed
4   cups shredded cooked chicken
3   cups fresh yellow corn kernels (about 6 ears)
2   cups uncooked, shelled frozen edamame (green soybeans)
1   (13.5-oz.) can unsweetened coconut milk
1   Tbsp. curry powder
2   tsp. table salt
1   tsp. pepper
Toppings: toasted coconut, green onion strips, peanuts, lime wedges

1. Sauté first 3 ingredients in hot oil in a large Dutch oven or stockpot over medium-high heat 5 minutes or until tender; add garlic, and sauté 1 minute. Add broth and next 9 ingredients; bring to a boil, stirring often. Reduce heat to medium, and simmer, stirring occasionally, 20 to 25 minutes or until vegetables are tender. Serve with desired toppings.

corn chowder with poblano

makes 4 servings · hands-on time 20 min. · total time 56 min.

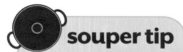

souper tip

Frozen creamed corn and fat-free cream cheese are the base for this spicy-sweet, creamy chowder. Enjoy a cupful for a light lunch, or serve it alongside a sandwich for a more substantial supper.

1 large poblano pepper, cut in half lengthwise
1 (20-oz.) tube frozen creamed corn, thawed
1½ cups 1% low-fat or fat-free milk
¼ tsp. table salt
⅛ to ¼ tsp. ground red pepper
¼ tsp. ground cumin
1½ to 2 cups reduced-sodium fat-free chicken broth
½ (8-oz.) package fat-free cream cheese, softened
Garnishes: thinly sliced jalapeño pepper strips, ground black pepper

1. Preheat broiler. Broil poblano pepper halves, skin side up, on an aluminum foil-lined baking sheet 6 inches from heat 5 to 6 minutes or until pepper looks blistered. Fold aluminum foil over pepper to seal, and let stand 10 minutes. Peel pepper; remove and discard seeds. Coarsely chop pepper; set aside.

2. Bring creamed corn and next 4 ingredients to a boil in a 3-qt. saucepan over medium-high heat, stirring mixture constantly. Reduce heat to low, and simmer, stirring often, 10 minutes.

3. Stir 1½ cups chicken broth into mixture. Whisk in softened cream cheese and chopped poblano pepper; cook, whisking often, 5 minutes or until cream cheese melts and mixture is thoroughly heated. Whisk in additional chicken broth, if necessary, to reach desired consistency. Serve chowder immediately.

corn-and-zucchini queso chowder

makes 11 cups · hands-on time 40 min. · total time 1 hour

¼ cup butter
1   cup finely chopped red
    bell pepper
1   cup finely chopped onion
3   poblano peppers, seeded
    and finely chopped
2   garlic cloves, minced
2   cups frozen whole kernel
    corn, thawed
2   cups chopped zucchini
¼   tsp. ground cumin
2   (14-oz.) cans low-sodium
    fat-free chicken broth

⅓ cup all-purpose flour
1½ cups milk
1   cup half-and-half
1   cup (4 oz.) freshly shredded
    asadero cheese*
1   cup (4 oz.) freshly shredded
    sharp Cheddar cheese
½   tsp. kosher salt
Toppings: chopped cooked
    bacon, shredded Cheddar
    cheese, diced red onion

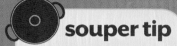

souper tip

Shredding the asadero and sharp Cheddar cheeses from blocks of cheese makes all the difference here. Pre-shredded cheeses just won't melt as well.

1. Melt butter in a Dutch oven over medium-high heat; add bell pepper and next 3 ingredients, and sauté 4 to 5 minutes or until tender. Add corn, zucchini, and cumin, and sauté 5 minutes or until tender. Gradually stir in broth, stirring to loosen particles from bottom of Dutch oven. Bring to a boil; cover, reduce heat to low, and simmer 15 minutes.

2. Whisk together flour and next 2 ingredients. Stir into corn mixture, and cook over medium heat, stirring constantly, 5 minutes or until thickened. Reduce heat to low.

3. Add asadero cheese, Cheddar cheese, and salt, and cook, stirring constantly, until cheeses melt and mixture is thoroughly heated. Serve with desired toppings.

* Monterey Jack cheese may be substituted.

Chilled Mexican-Style
Salsa Soup, page 186

chilled
soups

chilled strawberry soup

makes about 4 cups · hands-on time 10 min. · total time 2 hours, 10 min.

souper tip

See page 248 for a delicious Strawberry-Buttermilk Ice Cream made with 2 cups of this soup.

This refreshing soup offers a splash of excitement with the addition of Riesling. Serve it for a first course or a lighter dessert.

3 cups sliced fresh strawberries
1 cup plain Greek yogurt
½ cup Riesling
⅓ cup sugar
Garnishes: olive oil, freshly ground pepper, sliced fresh strawberries

1. Process strawberries, Greek yogurt, Riesling, and sugar in a blender or food processor until smooth, stopping to scrape down sides as needed. Cover and chill 2 hours.

chilled watermelon soup

makes 4 cups · hands-on time 15 min. · total time 1 hour, 15 min.

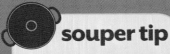

souper tip

For the best flavor, purchase watermelons grown locally. Look for melons that are free of dents, bruises, and cuts. Look at the bottom of the melon; it should be yellow or lighter in color. Tap the melon; it should sound hollow. Pick it up and feel for heaviness. Ripe watermelons are heavier than they look.

Fresh lime juice adds tang to this soup, and honey contributes a little extra sweetness. If your watermelon is good and sweet, omit the honey.

4	cups seeded watermelon cubes	1	tsp. chopped fresh mint
⅓	cup apple juice	¼	to ½ tsp. ground ginger
2	Tbsp. fresh lime juice	1	Tbsp. honey (optional)
		⅓	cup plain nonfat yogurt

1. Process first 5 ingredients and honey, if desired, in a blender or food processor until smooth, stopping to scrape down sides as needed. Cover and chill 1 hour. Serve in individual bowls with a dollop of yogurt.

chilled carrot soup

makes 5 cups · hands-on time 30 min. · total time 6 hours, 5 min.

3 cups peeled and diced baking potatoes
2 cups diced carrots
1½ cups chopped leeks
1 (32-oz.) container chicken broth
1 Tbsp. jarred chicken soup base

1 cup half-and-half
½ tsp. salt
¼ tsp. ground white pepper
Garnish: finely shredded carrots

1. Combine first 5 ingredients in a Dutch oven; bring to a boil over medium-high heat. Cover, reduce heat to low, and simmer 10 minutes or until vegetables are tender. Cool 10 minutes.

2. Puree vegetable mixture, in batches, in a blender until smooth. Transfer puree to a large bowl; whisk in half-and-half, salt, and white pepper until blended. Let cool 1 hour; cover and chill 4 to 48 hours.

3. Add salt and pepper to taste. Serve in chilled cups.

Note: We tested with Superior Touch Better Than Bouillon Chicken Base.

souper tip

When leeks are grown, soil is piled high around them, causing dirt and sand to lodge deep inside the layers. To clean leeks: Remove and discard root ends and dark green tops of leeks. Cut in half lengthwise, and rinse thoroughly under cold running water to remove grit and sand. Slice or chop as needed for the recipe.

HOW TO:

prepare fresh fruits and veggies

Fresh produce is the star of chilled soups. Here's how to prepare a few key ingredients.

avocados

1. Insert a chef's knife into the top of the avocado where the stem was, and press down until you reach the pit. Holding the knife steady, rotate the avocado so the knife moves around the pit, cutting the entire avocado.

2. Remove the knife, then slowly and gently twist the two sides away from each other to separate.

3. Strike the pit, and pierce it with the blade of the knife. Then twist and remove the knife; the pit will come with it.

4. Using the knife's tip, cut the flesh in horizontal and vertical rows. Do not cut through the skin.

5. Remove the flesh gently with a spoon.

cucumbers

1. Remove the skin with a vegetable peeler.
2. Cut about ½ inch from each end of the cucumber.
3. Slice the cucumber in half lengthwise. If desired, gently scoop out the seeds from both halves with a spoon.

peaches

If the peach is still firm, you can remove the skin using a vegetable peeler or a paring knife. If the fruit is soft, you can remove the skin by blanching:

1. Cut an "X" in the bottom of each peach, being careful to cut just through the skin.
2. Bring a large pot of water to a boil, and drop in the peaches. Cook for 20 seconds to 1 minute. The riper the peaches, the less time they will need.
3. Remove the peaches from the water with a slotted spoon, and place them in a bowl filled with ice water.
4. Using a paring knife or your fingers, remove the skin, which should slip right off.

avocado soup with marinated shrimp

makes 8 to 10 appetizer servings · hands-on time 15 min. · total time 1 hour, 30 min.

3 large avocados, cut into chunks
2 (14-oz.) cans vegetable broth
¼ tsp. ground red pepper
1 tsp. table salt, divided
½ cup buttermilk
4 Tbsp. fresh lemon juice, divided
¼ cup Riesling (optional)
½ lb. medium-size peeled, cooked shrimp
1 Tbsp. olive oil
1 tsp. lemon zest
Garnish: chopped fresh chives

souper tip

Instead of bowls, consider using martini glasses, shot glasses, or other fun glassware to serve this soup.

1. Process first 3 ingredients and ¼ tsp. salt in a blender until smooth, stopping to scrape down sides as needed.

2. Transfer avocado mixture to a bowl; stir in buttermilk, 3 Tbsp. lemon juice, and, if desired, wine until smooth. Place plastic wrap directly on soup, and chill at least 1 hour or up to 4 hours.

3. During last 15 minutes of chill time for avocado mixture, combine shrimp, olive oil, lemon zest, and remaining 1 Tbsp. lemon juice and ¾ tsp. salt, and let stand 15 minutes.

4. Ladle soup into small bowls, and top each with shrimp.

creamy cucumber soup

makes about 2 qt. · hands-on time 20 min. · total time 4 hours, 20 min.

souper tip

English, or hothouse, cucumbers have thin skins, few seeds, and mild flavor. English cucumbers are sold wrapped in plastic, rather than coated in wax.

¾ cup chicken broth
3 green onions
2 Tbsp. white vinegar
½ tsp. table salt
¼ tsp. ground black pepper
3 large English cucumbers (about 2½ lb.), peeled, seeded, chopped, and divided

3 cups fat-free Greek yogurt*
Garnishes: toasted slivered almonds, freshly ground pepper, chopped red bell pepper

1. Process chicken broth, green onions, vinegar, salt, pepper, and half of chopped cucumbers in a food processor until smooth, stopping to scrape down sides as needed.

2. Add yogurt, and pulse until blended. Pour into a large bowl; stir in remaining chopped cucumbers. Cover and chill 4 to 24 hours. Season with salt to taste just before serving.

*Plain low-fat yogurt may be substituted. Decrease chicken broth to ½ cup.

chilled zucchini soup

makes 6½ cups · hands-on time 15 min. · total time 2 hours, 44 min.

....

This soup is full of fresh flavors—just the ticket for a summer lunch or light supper. Make it ahead, and store in an airtight container in the refrigerator up to two days.

½ cup diced sweet onion
½ cup diced fennel bulb
3 garlic cloves, sliced
1 Tbsp. olive oil
5 cups diced zucchini (about 2½ lb.)
2 cups organic vegetable broth

½ cup whole buttermilk
2 tsp. kosher salt
2 tsp. Champagne vinegar
1 tsp. lemon zest
1 tsp. fresh lemon juice

1. Sauté onion, fennel, and garlic in hot oil in a large Dutch oven over medium-high heat 5 minutes; add zucchini, and sauté 3 minutes. Stir in vegetable broth and 1 cup water; bring to a simmer. Cook 15 minutes or until vegetables are tender. Remove from heat.

2. Process with a handheld blender 4 minutes or until smooth. Stir in buttermilk, salt, vinegar, lemon zest, and lemon juice. Let stand at room temperature 15 minutes. Cover and chill 2 hours or up to 2 days.

watercress-buttermilk soup

makes 8 to 10 servings · hands-on time: 20 min. · total time: 40 min.

Look for watercress with small, bright green leaves and thin stems to make this peppery soup.

1	medium leek
2	Tbsp. butter
1	garlic clove, minced
6	cups organic chicken or vegetable broth
1	large russet potato (about 1 lb.), peeled and cut into 1-inch cubes
1	(5-oz.) package fresh baby spinach
2	(4-oz.) packages watercress (about 16 loosely packed cups)

1 tsp. kosher salt
½ tsp. finely ground black pepper
Pinch of ground red pepper
2 cups whole buttermilk
1 tsp. fresh lemon juice
Garnishes: buttermilk, watercress sprigs, chopped fresh chives

1. Remove and discard root end and dark green top of leek. Cut in half lengthwise, and rinse under cold running water to remove grit and sand. Thinly slice leek.

2. Melt butter in a Dutch oven over medium heat; add leek, and sauté 8 to 10 minutes or until tender. Add garlic, and sauté 1 minute.

3. Add broth and potato; cover and cook, stirring occasionally, 20 minutes or until potato is tender. Remove from heat, and add spinach and next 4 ingredients, stirring until spinach is wilted.

4. Puree soup with a blender until smooth; pour into a large bowl. Whisk in buttermilk and lemon juice; add salt and pepper to taste. Serve chilled or at room temperature.

chunky tomato-fruit gazpacho

makes about 9 cups · hands-on time 30 min. · total time 2 hours, 30 min.

- 2 **cups finely diced cantaloupe**
- 2 **cups finely diced honeydew melon**
- 2 **cups finely diced tomatoes**
- 1 **mango, finely diced**
- 2 **salad cucumbers, finely diced**
- 1 **jalapeño pepper, seeded and finely chopped**

- 1 **cup finely diced peaches**
- 2 **cups fresh orange juice**
- ½ **cup finely chopped sweet onion**
- ¼ **cup chopped fresh basil**
- 3 **Tbsp. chopped fresh mint**
- 3 **Tbsp. fresh lemon juice**
- 1 **tsp. sugar**
- ½ **tsp. salt**
- **Garnish: fresh basil sprigs**

1. Combine first 14 ingredients in a large bowl. Cover and chill 2 to 24 hours.

souper tip

The mango, melon, and peaches, along with the cucumbers, give the gazpacho a sweet spin. Don't seed the jalapeño if you like a soup with more zip. Prepare it the day before to allow the flavors to develop fully.

easy toppings for chilled soups

Chilled soups lend themselves to creative toppers. Here are a few ideas that add flavor and texture.

Yogurt or Sour Cream:

Place about ½ cup yogurt or sour cream in a zip-top plastic bag, and seal. Snip off a corner of the bottom of the bag with scissors to create a small hole. Squeeze the yogurt or sour cream through the hole to make interesting designs on the top of each serving of soup.

You can use a smooth back-and-forth motion and move the plastic bag over the soup to create a zigzag pattern. Or you can hold the bag steady in one place and squeeze to create large and small polka dots on the top of the soup.

To make heart shapes, use a circular motion to make several small spirals on top of the soup. Then use a skewer or tip of a paring knife and run the point through the center of each spiral to create heart shapes. Or, if you're in a hurry, a simple dollop is always a nice touch.

Fresh Herbs:

Use sprigs of fresh herbs or finely chopped fresh herbs as garnishes. Basil, oregano, cilantro, and chives are often good choices for chilled vegetable soups, while chopped fresh mint or mint sprigs are delicious on creamy fruit soups.

Fresh Fruits or Vegetables:

If you're making a chilled soup, set aside a few pieces of the fruit or vegetable called for in the recipe to use as a garnish. For example, a thin slice of a fresh peach or a paper-thin cucumber slice, a sliced fresh strawberry, or a small pile of shredded carrot are all perfect for toppers. For berry soups, you can top with a few small whole berries. Depending on the flavors in the soup, fresh lemon or lime zest also makes a nice garnish and adds a punch of flavor.

Croutons:

Use commercial croutons or make your own with toasted cubes of bread. For sweet fruit soups, you can make croutons with toasted cubes of pound cake or some type of dessert bread, such as banana bread.

summer gazpacho

makes 4 to 6 servings · hands-on time 25 min. · total time 25 min.

souper tip

Chill the soup bowls in the refrigerator for about 30 minutes or 15 minutes in the freezer before serving.

Serve this immediately on busy weeknights for a fresh and light meal. Or make ahead and chill to let the flavors brighten even more.

1 medium-size red heirloom tomato
1 cup diced seedless watermelon
1 cup diced strawberries
1 Kirby cucumber, diced
1 cup diced peaches
1 jalapeño pepper, seeded and minced
1½ cups fresh orange juice
⅓ cup finely chopped sweet onion
1½ Tbsp. chopped fresh basil
1½ Tbsp. chopped fresh mint
2 Tbsp. extra virgin olive oil
1 Tbsp. red wine vinegar
½ tsp. kosher salt
Avocado West Indies Salad
Whole-grain crackers (optional)

1. Cut tomato in half; gently squeeze to remove seeds. Discard seeds, and chop tomato. Combine tomato and next 12 ingredients in a large pitcher. Serve immediately, or cover and chill up to 24 hours.

2. Meanwhile, prepare Avocado West Indies Salad. Spoon gazpacho into bowls. Top with Avocado West Indies Salad. Serve with crackers, if desired.

avocado west indies salad

makes 4 to 6 servings · hands-on time 8 min. · total time 8 min.

This crab salad is good by itself or served over Summer Gazpacho for a light, fresh meal.

- 1 medium avocado, chopped
- 8 oz. fresh jumbo lump crabmeat, drained
- ⅓ cup diced sweet onion
- 2 Tbsp. chopped fresh basil
- 3 Tbsp. apple cider vinegar
- 3 Tbsp. extra virgin olive oil
- ¼ tsp. kosher salt
- ¼ tsp. freshly ground pepper

1. Gently stir together all ingredients. Serve immediately, or chill up to 2 hours.

chilled mexican-style salsa soup

makes 4 servings · hands-on time 17 min. · total time 1 hour, 17 min.

2 cups grape or cherry tomatoes

1½ cups green bell pepper, cut into 1-inch pieces

1 cup vegetable juice (such as V8)

¾ cup diced seeded peeled cucumber

⅓ cup chopped red onion

6 Tbsp. fresh lime juice (about 3 medium limes)

¼ cup firmly packed cilantro leaves

2 tsp. paprika

¾ tsp. table salt

¼ tsp. ground red pepper (optional)

¼ cup low-fat sour cream (optional)

1. Place first 9 ingredients and, if desired, ground red pepper, in a blender; process until finely minced. Cover and chill thoroughly. Top each serving with 1 Tbsp. sour cream, if desired.

tropical fruit soup

makes 12 cups · hands-on time 25 min. · total time 55 min.

1 fresh pineapple, peeled, cored, and chopped

2 fresh mangoes, peeled and chopped

3 kiwifruit, peeled and chopped

¼ lb. green seedless grapes, halved (about 1 cup)

¼ tsp. ground cardamom

4 cups white grape juice

Garnish: fresh mint sprigs

1. Stir together first 4 ingredients in a large bowl. Sprinkle with cardamom. Pour grape juice over fruit, stirring gently. Cover and chill 30 minutes.

Pam's Country Crust
Bread, page 204

side fixin's and serve-alongs

buttermilk cornbread

makes 8 servings · hands-on time 5 min. · total time 35 min.

souper tip

Serve this Southern staple with soups, stews, or salads. Plan to pop it in the oven when guests arrive, so you can enjoy it hot.

1¼ cups all-purpose flour
1 cup plus 3 Tbsp. plain white cornmeal
¼ cup sugar
1 Tbsp. baking powder
1 tsp. table salt
¼ cup butter, melted
2 large eggs
1 cup buttermilk

1. Preheat oven to 400°. Lightly grease an 8-inch cast-iron skillet, and heat in oven 5 minutes.

2. Meanwhile, whisk together first 5 ingredients in a bowl; whisk in melted butter. Add eggs and buttermilk, whisking just until smooth.

3. Pour batter into hot skillet. Bake at 400° for 30 to 33 minutes or until golden brown.

texas cornbread sticks

makes 16 sticks · hands-on time 10 min. · total time 28 min.

souper tip

When combined with moisture and an acid, such as buttermilk, baking soda produces carbon dioxide bubbles that cause baked goods to rise. Be sure to check for an expiration date, because baking soda starts to weaken after six months. To test it for freshness, just stir 1 teaspoon baking soda into ¼ cup vinegar. An immediate fizz means it's still strong.

1   cup yellow cornmeal
½   cup all-purpose flour
1   tsp. table salt
¼   tsp. baking soda
¼   tsp. ground red pepper

1¼   cups buttermilk
¼   cup butter, melted
1   large egg
1   Tbsp. vegetable oil

1. Preheat oven to 450°. Combine first 5 ingredients; make a well in center. Stir together buttermilk, butter, and egg. Add to flour mixture, stirring just until moistened.

2. Heat cast-iron cornstick pans in oven 5 minutes or until hot. Remove pans from oven, and brush lightly with vegetable oil. Spoon batter evenly into hot pans.

3. Bake at 450° for 18 minutes or until golden brown. Remove from pans immediately; cool slightly on wire racks.

thin-crisp cornbread

makes 4 to 6 servings · hands-on time 15 min. · total time 27 min.

- ¾ cup plus 2 Tbsp. stone-ground cornmeal
- 6 Tbsp. all-purpose flour
- ¼ tsp. baking soda
- 2 tsp. baking powder
- ½ tsp. table salt
- ¾ cup buttermilk
- ¼ cup canola oil
- 2 Tbsp. honey
- 1 large egg
- 1 tsp. canola oil

1. Preheat oven to 450°. Combine first 5 ingredients in a bowl. Stir in buttermilk and next 3 ingredients until well blended.

2. Heat 1 tsp. oil in a 9-inch cast-iron skillet over medium-high heat. Pour batter into skillet.

3. Bake at 450° for 10 to 12 minutes or until golden brown.

chile-corn griddle cakes

makes 10 (4-inch) cakes · hands-on time 10 min. · total time 18 min.

The corn adds great texture, and the green chiles contribute a touch of heat to these griddle cakes.

1   **cup frozen whole kernel corn, thawed**
1   **cup cornmeal mix**
½   **cup buttermilk**
½   **cup boiling water**
1   **(4.5-oz.) can chopped green chiles, undrained**
1   **Tbsp. vegetable oil**
¼   **tsp. ground cumin**
  Butter

1. Whisk together first 7 ingredients, whisking just until dry ingredients are moistened. (Batter will be thin.)

2. Spoon batter by level ¼ cupfuls onto a hot (375°) greased griddle or a greased nonstick skillet over medium-high heat. Cook, in batches, 3 to 4 minutes or until tops are covered with bubbles and edges look slightly dry and cooked; turn and cook until done. Serve with butter.

parmesan-pepper cornbread biscotti

makes about 1½ dozen · hands-on time 15 min. · total time 1 hour, 30 min.

2 (6-oz.) packages buttermilk cornbread-and-muffin mix
1 cup (4 oz.) freshly grated Parmesan cheese, divided
2 tsp. freshly ground pepper
¾ tsp. chopped fresh rosemary
¼ cup cold butter, cut into pieces
3 large eggs, divided
¼ cup buttermilk
Parchment paper

1. Preheat oven to 350°. Combine cornbread mix, ¾ cup Parmesan cheese, and next 2 ingredients in a food processor bowl. Add butter, and pulse 5 to 6 times or until crumbly.

2. Whisk together 2 eggs and buttermilk. With processor running, gradually add egg mixture through food chute, and process just until well moistened. (Batter will be thick.)

3. Spread dough into a 12- x 4-inch rectangle on a parchment paper-lined baking sheet using lightly greased hands. Lightly beat remaining egg; brush over dough. Sprinkle with remaining cheese.

4. Bake at 350° for 20 minutes or until pale golden brown and firm. Let cool on baking sheet on a wire rack 10 minutes. Reduce oven temperature to 300°.

5. Gently slide loaf (on parchment paper) onto a cutting board, and cut loaf diagonally into ½-inch-thick slices using a serrated knife. Place slices, cut sides down, on a baking sheet lined with a new sheet of parchment paper.

6. Bake at 300° for 15 to 20 minutes on each side or until golden and crisp. Let cool on baking sheet on wire rack 15 minutes. Serve warm. Store in an airtight container up to 3 days, or freeze up to 2 weeks.

Note: We tested with Martha White Buttermilk Cornbread & Muffin Mix.

HOW TO:

care for your cast-iron skillet

Cast-iron skillets can be passed on for generations if they're cared for properly. Here's how.

Seasoning is the process of oiling and heating cast iron to protect its porous surface from moisture. When the pan is heated, the oil is absorbed, creating a nonstick surface.

1

Rinse the skillet in hot sudsy water. Dry the skillet well with a towel.

2

Rub the skillet generously with vegetable oil, coating both the insides and the bottom of the skillet.

3

Place the skillet in an oven, and bake at 350° for 2 hours. Let the skillet cool, and pour off any excess oil. Repeat this process two or three times to season the skillet completely.

Follow these tips to help keep your cast-iron skillet in tip-top shape:

• Before cooking, apply vegetable oil to the cooking surface, and preheat the pan on low heat, increasing the temperature slowly.

• Because acids can corrode cast iron, remove any highly acidic foods (such as tomatoes) from the skillet as soon as the dish has finished cooking.

• As soon as you have removed the food from the skillet, scrub the pan while it's still warm but cool enough to handle with ease under hot water. Use a stiff brush or plastic scrubber. Kosher salt is also a good scrubbing agent for baked-on stains. The most important tip is to never use soap unless you're seasoning or reseasoning the pan.

• After scrubbing the pan under hot water, place on warm burner for a few minutes to dry. After it has dried, dribble a little bit of oil on the inside of the skillet to help it maintain the seasoning. Rub the oil all over the skillet with a paper towel so that the skillet shines. Let the skillet cool completely.

• To rid your skillet of rust stains, rub a handy rust eraser on the stain, and then re-season the pan. You can find rust erasers at hardware stores, bike shops, or woodworking shops. Or, use fine steel wool. Scrub the skillet with hot water, and then scour with fine steel wool again before drying and re-seasoning.

• Never marinate in cast iron. Acidic mixtures will damage the seasoning. Re-season if food particles start to stick, rust appears, or you experience a metallic taste.

• Never put a cast-iron skillet in the dishwasher. Moist environments will cause rust and damage the seasoning.

quick buttermilk biscuits

makes about 3 dozen · hands-on time 10 min. · total time 22 min.

It takes only three ingredients to make quick, from-scratch buttermilk biscuits. Fill biscuits with thinly sliced ham, if desired. To freeze these, place the unbaked biscuits on pans in freezer for 30 minutes or until frozen. Transfer frozen biscuits to zip-top plastic freezer bags, and freeze up to 3 months. Bake frozen biscuits at 425° on lightly greased baking sheets 14 to 16 minutes or until lightly browned.

1 **cup shortening**	1¾ **cups buttermilk**
4 **cups self-rising soft-wheat flour**	

1. Preheat oven to 425°. Cut shortening into flour with a pastry blender or with the back of a fork until crumbly. Add buttermilk, stirring just until dry ingredients are moistened.

2. Turn dough out onto a lightly floured surface, and knead lightly 4 to 5 times. Pat or roll dough to ¾-inch thickness, cut with a 1½-inch round cutter, and place on 2 lightly greased baking sheets.

3. Bake at 425° for 12 to 14 minutes or until lightly browned.

souper tip

better biscuits

- Spoon flour into a dry measuring cup, and level with the straight edge of a metal spatula. Don't use a liquid measuring cup.
- Shake the carton of buttermilk before measuring.
- If your hands are warm, run them under cold water (and thoroughly dry) before you knead the dough.
- Dust the work surface with all-purpose flour when rolling and shaping the dough.
- Cut straight down with a sharp biscuit cutter. Don't twist the cutter, or you'll seal the edges of the biscuit and reduce the rise. Ditto on using a glass—both sides of the cutter need to be open to allow air to exit as you press down.

green chile biscuits

makes 1 dozen · hands-on time 10 min. · total time 20 min.

2 cups all-purpose baking mix
1 cup (4 oz.) shredded Mexican four-cheese blend
1 (4.5-oz.) can chopped green chiles, drained
⅔ cup milk

1. Preheat oven to 450°. Stir together baking mix and remaining ingredients until a soft dough forms. Turn dough onto a lightly floured surface; knead 3 or 4 times.

2. Pat or roll dough to ½-inch thickness; cut with a 2½-inch round cutter, and place on an ungreased baking sheet.

3. Bake at 450° for 10 to 12 minutes or until biscuits are golden brown.

Note: We tested with Bisquick all-purpose baking mix.

fresh tomato biscuits

makes 10 biscuits · hands-on time 10 min. · total time 22 min.

These easy biscuits are divine when using fresh, in-season tomatoes.

¼ cup mayonnaise

¼ tsp. table salt

¼ tsp. coarsely ground pepper

¼ cup shredded fresh basil

1 (16.3-oz.) can refrigerated flaky biscuits

2 medium-size tomatoes, thinly sliced

1. Preheat oven to 400°. Combine first 4 ingredients. Set aside.

2. Press each biscuit into a 4-inch circle. Place biscuit circles on a lightly greased baking sheet.

3. Bake at 400° for 6 minutes. Spread each biscuit evenly with about 2 tsp. mayonnaise mixture. Top evenly with tomato slices. Bake at 400° for 6 more minutes or until mayonnaise mixture is bubbly. Serve immediately.

Note: We tested with Pillsbury Golden Layers Buttermilk Biscuits.

souper tip

You can prepare these using the recipe for Quick Buttermilk Biscuits on page 199, or use your favorite frozen biscuits when you're running short on time.

sorghum-oat bread

makes 2 loaves · hands-on time 45 min. · total time 4 hours, 20 min.

souper tip

Be sure the oat mixture has cooled before you mix it with the yeast. If it's too hot, it can kill the yeast, causing the bread not to rise.

2¼ cups boiling water
1 cup uncooked regular oats
¼ cup butter
½ cup firmly packed dark brown sugar
2 Tbsp. sorghum syrup
1 Tbsp. fresh lemon juice
½ cup warm water (100° to 110°)
1 Tbsp. active dry yeast
1 tsp. granulated sugar
4 cups bread flour
1½ cups whole wheat flour
1 Tbsp. table salt
1 tsp. ground cinnamon
2 Tbsp. butter, melted

1. Stir together first 3 ingredients in bowl of a heavy-duty electric stand mixer until butter melts. Stir in brown sugar and next 2 ingredients. Cool until lukewarm (20 to 30 minutes).

2. Meanwhile, stir together ½ cup warm water, yeast, and granulated sugar in a 1-cup glass measuring cup; let stand 5 minutes.

3. Stir together bread flour and next 3 ingredients in a medium bowl. Stir yeast mixture into oat mixture. Gradually add flour mixture to oat mixture, beating on low speed until well blended.

4. Sprinkle a flat surface generously with bread flour. Turn dough out, and knead until smooth and elastic (about 6 to 8 minutes), sprinkling surface with bread flour as needed. Place dough in a lightly greased large bowl, turning to grease top. Cover and let rise in a warm place (80° to 85°), about 1 hour or until doubled in bulk.

5. Punch dough down; turn out onto a lightly floured surface. Divide dough in half. Roll each half into an 18- x 9-inch rectangle. Starting at short end, tightly roll up each rectangle, jelly-roll fashion, pressing to seal edges as you roll. Pinch ends of dough to seal, and tuck ends under dough. Place each dough roll, seam side down, in a lightly greased 9- x 5-inch loaf pan. Cover and let rise in a warm place (80° to 85°), free from drafts, 1 hour or until doubled in bulk.

6. Preheat oven to 350°. Bake 30 to 35 minutes or until loaves are golden brown and sound hollow when tapped. Remove from pans to a wire rack, and brush loaves with melted butter. Cool completely (about 1 hour).

pam's country crust bread

makes 2 loaves · hands-on time 25 min. · total time 3 hours, 50 min.

souper tip

VARIATIONS
Country Crust Wheat Bread: Substitute 3 cups wheat flour for 3 cups bread flour.

Country Crust Cheese Bread: Sprinkle 1 cup (4 oz.) freshly shredded sharp Cheddar cheese onto each rectangle before rolling up.

2 (¼-oz.) envelopes active dry yeast
2 cups warm water (100° to 110°)
½ cup sugar
2 large eggs
¼ cup vegetable oil
1 Tbsp. table salt
1 Tbsp. fresh lemon juice
6 to 6½ cups bread flour
1 Tbsp. vegetable oil
1½ Tbsp. butter, melted

1. Combine yeast, warm water, and 2 tsp. sugar in bowl of a heavy-duty electric stand mixer; let stand 5 minutes. Stir in eggs, next 3 ingredients, 3 cups flour, and remaining sugar. Beat dough at medium speed, using paddle attachment, until smooth. Gradually beat in remaining 3 to 3½ cups flour until a soft dough forms.

2. Turn dough out onto a well-floured surface, and knead until smooth and elastic (about 8 to 10 minutes), sprinkling surface with flour as needed. Place dough in a lightly greased large bowl, turning to grease top. Cover and let rise in a warm place (80° to 85°), free from drafts, about 1 hour or until doubled in bulk.

3. Punch dough down; turn out onto a lightly floured surface. Divide dough in half.

4. Roll each dough half into an 18- x 9-inch rectangle. Starting at 1 short end, tightly roll up each rectangle, jelly-roll fashion, pressing to seal edges as you roll. Pinch ends of dough to seal, and tuck ends under dough. Place each dough roll, seam side down, in a lightly greased 9- x 5-inch loaf pan. Brush tops with oil. Cover and let rise in a warm place (80° to 85°), free from drafts, 1 hour or until doubled in bulk.

5. Preheat oven to 375°. Bake 25 to 30 minutes or until loaves are deep golden brown and sound hollow when tapped. Remove from pans to a wire rack, and brush loaves with melted butter. Let cool completely (about 1 hour).

rosemary focaccia bread

makes 10 to 12 servings · hands-on time 30 min. · total time 3 hours

1 (¼-oz.) envelope active dry yeast
1⅔ cups warm water (100° to 110°)
4½ cups bread flour
¼ cup extra virgin olive oil
1 Tbsp. table salt
2 Tbsp. fresh rosemary leaves, divided
3 Tbsp. extra virgin olive oil
1 tsp. kosher salt

1. Stir together yeast and warm water in bowl of a heavy-duty electric stand mixer; let stand 5 minutes.

2. Add bread flour, ¼ cup oil, and 1 Tbsp. table salt to yeast mixture. Beat on low speed, using paddle attachment, 10 seconds or until blended. Increase speed to medium. Beat 45 seconds or until dough is smooth. Add 1 Tbsp. rosemary. Replace paddle attachment with dough hook; increase speed to medium-high, and beat 4 minutes. (Dough will be sticky.)

3. Turn dough onto a floured surface, and knead until smooth and elastic (about 1 minute). Place in a greased bowl, turning to coat. Cover dough with plastic wrap, and let rise in a warm place (80° to 85°), free from drafts, 1 hour or until doubled in bulk.

4. Press dough into a well greased 15- x 10-inch jelly-roll pan, pressing to about ¼-inch thickness. Cover with a kitchen towel, and let rise in a warm place (80° to 85°), free from drafts. 1 hour.

5. Preheat oven to 475°. Press handle of a wooden spoon into dough to make indentations at 1-inch intervals; drizzle with 3 Tbsp. oil. Sprinkle with kosher salt and remaining 1 Tbsp. rosemary. Bake 14 to 16 minutes or until top is light brown. Remove from pan to a wire rack, and cool 10 minutes.

extra cheesy grilled cheese

makes 4 sandwiches · hands-on time 10 min. · total time 26 min.

¼ cup butter, softened
1 Tbsp. grated Parmesan cheese
8 Italian bread slices

4 (¾-oz.) provolone cheese slices
4 (¾-oz.) mozzarella cheese slices

1. Stir together butter and Parmesan cheese in a small bowl.

2. Spread 1½ tsp. butter mixture on 1 side of each bread slice. Place 4 bread slices, buttered sides down, on wax paper. Top with provolone and mozzarella cheeses; top with remaining bread slices, buttered sides up.

3. Cook sandwiches, in batches, on a hot griddle or in a nonstick skillet over medium heat, gently pressing with a spatula, 4 minutes on each side or until golden brown and cheese is melted.

quick quesadillas

makes 6 appetizer servings · hands-on time 16 min. · total time 28 min.

6 (6-inch) fajita-size flour
   tortillas
¾ cup (3 oz.) shredded
   Monterey Jack cheese
¾ cup (3 oz.) shredded
   Cheddar cheese
1 (4-oz.) can chopped green
   chiles, undrained

3 medium plum tomatoes,
   chopped
Vegetable cooking spray
Sour cream
Salsa

souper tip

For easier flipping, place one tortilla in the skillet, top with fillings, and fold in half. Cook as directed, and cut into three triangles.

1. Place 1 flour tortilla in a small lightly greased nonstick skillet over low heat. Sprinkle with 2 Tbsp. each of shredded cheeses. Spread with 1 Tbsp. chiles; sprinkle with 3 Tbsp. tomatoes. Top with 1 tortilla, and coat with cooking spray.

2. Cook quesadilla over low heat 2 to 3 minutes on each side or until golden. Remove from skillet; keep warm.

3. Repeat procedure with remaining tortillas, cheeses, chiles, and tomatoes. Cut each quesadilla into 6 triangles. Serve with sour cream and salsa.

quick & easy ideas for sides

The beauty of a bowl of soup is that it can be a one-dish meal, and you don't need to spend much time on side dishes.

These creative ideas require nothing further than a quick stop at the supermarket deli or a glance into your pantry.

Chips and Crackers: tortilla chips, corn chips, pita chips, bagel chips, saltine crackers, oyster crackers, whole-wheat crackers, cheese crackers, pretzel rods, cheese straws

Breads: cornbread from supermarket deli, French baguette, focaccia, sourdough bread, whole-wheat rolls, toasted bagels, frozen biscuits, frozen rolls, refrigerated breadsticks

Salads and Veggies: packaged coleslaw mix, coleslaw from supermarket deli, salad from supermarket salad bar, bagged salad greens, baby carrots, celery sticks, fresh veggies with Ranch-style dip or hummus for dipping

Fruit salads and fresh fruit: pre-cut fresh fruit from produce section, fresh fruit from supermarket salad bar, canned fruit, frozen fruit

You can throw these together while your soup is simmering.

- **Berry-Lemon Salad:** Top fresh berries with a spoonful of lemon yogurt.
- **Balsamic Strawberries:** Top sliced strawberries with a splash of balsamic vinegar.
- **Minted Melon:** Top fresh melon cubes with a tablespoon of fresh mint and a splash of orange juice.
- **Pepper Cheese Toasts:** Sprinkle shredded Monterey Jack cheese with peppers over ½-inch-thick slices of French bread baguette and bake at 350° for 5 minutes or until cheese melts.
- **Sesame Bread:** Combine about 2 Tbsp. butter, 2 tsp. sesame seeds, and ¼ tsp. pepper, and spread over slices of French bread. Broil 4 to 5 minutes or until butter mixture is bubbly.

lemon-apple coleslaw

makes 4 servings · hands-on time 15 min. · total time 1 hour, 15 min.

1 small cabbage, shredded (8 cups)
2 apples, chopped
2 carrots, shredded
⅓ cup mayonnaise
1 Tbsp. sugar
2 Tbsp. minced onion
1 tsp. lemon zest
2 Tbsp. fresh lemon juice
¼ tsp. table salt
¼ tsp. freshly ground pepper

1. Combine cabbage, apples, and carrots in a large bowl.

2. Whisk together mayonnaise and next 6 ingredients; toss with cabbage mixture. Cover and chill 1 hour.

cranberry-almond coleslaw

makes 8 servings · hands-on time 15 min. · total time 15 min.

¼ cup apple cider vinegar
2 Tbsp. Dijon mustard
2 Tbsp. honey
¾ tsp. table salt
¼ tsp. freshly ground pepper
¼ cup canola oil
2 (10-oz.) packages shredded coleslaw mix
1 cup chopped smoked almonds
¾ cup sweetened dried cranberries
4 green onions, sliced
2 celery ribs, sliced

1. Whisk together first 5 ingredients. Gradually add oil in a slow, steady stream, whisking constantly until blended.

2. Stir together coleslaw mix and next 4 ingredients in a large bowl; add vinegar mixture, tossing to coat.

Cranberry-Almond
Coleslaw

broccoli slaw with candied pecans

makes 6 servings · hands-on time 15 min. · total time 1 hour, 15 min.

- 1 lb. fresh broccoli
- 1 cup mayonnaise
- ½ cup thinly sliced green onions
- ⅓ cup sugar
- ⅓ cup red wine vinegar
- 1 tsp. table salt
- 1 tsp. lemon zest
- ¼ tsp. ground red pepper
- ½ small head napa cabbage (about 1 lb.), thinly sliced*
- ½ cup golden raisins
- 1 (3.5-oz.) package roasted glazed pecan pieces

souper tip

You can substitute dark-skinned raisins, dried cranberries, or chopped dates in place of the golden raisins used in this recipe.

1. Cut broccoli florets from stems; separate florets into small pieces using a paring knife. Peel away tough outer layer of stems; finely chop stems.

2. Whisk together mayonnaise and next 6 ingredients in a large bowl; add cabbage, raisins, and broccoli, and stir to coat. Cover and chill 1 hour. Stir in pecans just before serving.

* 1 (16-oz.) package coleslaw mix may be substituted.

spinach-apple salad with maple-cider vinaigrette

makes 8 servings · hands-on time 20 min. · total time 50 min.

The pecans may be made up to 1 week ahead. Store in an airtight container. You can make the vinaigrette up to 3 days ahead. Cover and chill until ready to serve.

Sugared Curried Pecans
1   (6-oz.) package pecan halves
2   Tbsp. butter, melted
3   Tbsp. sugar
¼   tsp. ground ginger
⅛   tsp. curry powder
⅛   tsp. kosher salt
⅛   tsp. ground red pepper

Maple-Cider Vinaigrette
⅓   cup cider vinegar
2   Tbsp. pure maple syrup
1   Tbsp. Dijon mustard
¼   tsp. kosher salt
¼   tsp. freshly ground pepper
⅔   cup olive oil

Salad
1   (10-oz.) package fresh baby spinach, thoroughly washed
1   Gala apple, thinly sliced
1   small red onion, thinly sliced
1   (4-oz.) package crumbled goat cheese

1. Prepare Pecans: Preheat oven to 350°. Toss pecans in butter. Stir together sugar and next 4 ingredients in a bowl; add pecans, tossing to coat. Spread in a single layer in a nonstick aluminum foil-lined pan. Bake 10 to 13 minutes or until lightly browned and toasted. Cool in pan on a wire rack 20 minutes; separate pecans with a fork.

2. Prepare Vinaigrette: Whisk together cider vinegar and next 4 ingredients. Gradually whisk in oil until well blended.

3. Prepare Salad: Combine spinach and next 3 ingredients in a bowl. Drizzle with desired amount of Maple-Cider Vinaigrette; toss to coat. Sprinkle with pecans. Serve salad with any remaining vinaigrette.

harvest salad

makes 6 to 8 servings · hands-on time 15 min. · total time 50 min.

souper tip

When choosing butternut squash, look for one that has no cracks or soft spots and is heavy for its size.

1   large butternut squash
2   Tbsp. olive oil
2   Tbsp. honey
1   tsp. kosher salt
½   tsp. freshly ground pepper
1   (8-oz.) bottle poppy seed dressing
¼   cup fresh or frozen cranberries

2   (4-oz.) packages gourmet mixed salad greens
4   oz. goat cheese, crumbled
¾   cup lightly salted, roasted pecan halves
6   bacon slices, cooked and crumbled

1. Preheat oven to 400°. Peel and seed butternut squash; cut into ¾-inch cubes. Toss together squash, olive oil, and next 3 ingredients in a large bowl; place in a single layer in a lightly greased aluminum foil-lined 15- x 10-inch jelly-roll pan. Bake 20 to 25 minutes or until squash is tender and begins to brown, stirring once after 10 minutes. Remove from oven, and cool in pan 10 minutes.

2. Meanwhile, pulse poppy seed dressing and cranberries in a blender 3 to 4 times or until cranberries are coarsely chopped.

3. Toss together squash, gourmet salad greens, and next 3 ingredients on a large serving platter. Serve with dressing mixture.

creamy potato salad

makes 8 servings · hands-on time 16 min. · total time 39 min.

1½ lb. baking potatoes, peeled
⅓ cup mayonnaise
1 Tbsp. white vinegar
2 tsp. spicy brown mustard
¼ tsp. table salt
¼ tsp. freshly ground
   pepper
½ cup chopped green onions
   (4 onions)

¼ cup sweet or dill pickle
   relish
2 hard-cooked large eggs,
   finely shredded
⅛ tsp. freshly ground
   pepper (optional)
Sliced green onions (optional)
Chopped fresh parsley
   (optional)

1. Place potatoes in water to cover. Bring to a boil; cook 16 to 18 minutes or until tender. Drain; cool 15 minutes. Cut into cubes.

2. Combine mayonnaise and next 4 ingredients in a large bowl. Add potato, onions, relish, and eggs; toss to coat. Serve immediately, or cover and chill. Sprinkle with ⅛ tsp. pepper, green onions, and parsley, if desired, just before serving.

lemony potato salad

makes 6 servings · hands-on time 10 min. · total time 50 min.

This bright, fresh potato salad recipe features a tangy vinaigrette made with olive oil, lemon juice, and dry mustard.

2	lb. red potatoes, cut into eighths	½	tsp. dry mustard
¼	cup olive oil	¼	tsp. freshly ground pepper
3	Tbsp. fresh lemon juice	3	green onions, thinly sliced
¾	tsp. table salt	2	Tbsp. chopped fresh parsley

1. Bring potatoes and salted cold water to cover to a boil in a large Dutch oven; boil 15 to 17 minutes or just until tender. Drain and let cool 5 minutes.

2. Whisk together olive oil and next 4 ingredients in a large bowl. Add warm potatoes, green onions, and parsley; toss to coat. Serve at room temperature or chilled.

from-scratch oven fries

makes 4 servings · hands-on time 20 min. · total time 1 hour

souper tip

VARIATIONS

Buffalo Oven Fries:
Omit salt. Toss 2 tsp. mesquite seasoning, 1 tsp. hot sauce, ½ tsp. celery salt, and ½ tsp. garlic powder with potatoes and vegetable oil; bake as directed. Serve with blue cheese dressing and hot wing sauce, if desired.

Italian-Parmesan Oven Fries: Toss 2 tsp. freshly ground Italian seasoning with potato mixture, and bake as directed. Sprinkle warm fries with 2 Tbsp. grated Parmesan cheese. Serve with warm marinara sauce, if desired. Note: We tested with McCormick Italian Herb Seasoning Grinder.

Don't be afraid to sprinkle the fries with different seasoning blends instead of salt for a new twist.

1½ lb. medium-size baking potatoes, peeled and cut into ½-inch-thick strips

1 Tbsp. vegetable oil
½ tsp. kosher or table salt
Ketchup (optional)

1. Preheat oven to 450°. Rinse potatoes in cold water. Drain and pat dry. Toss together potatoes, oil, and salt in a large bowl.

2. Place a lightly greased wire rack in a jelly-roll pan. Arrange potatoes in a single layer on wire rack.

3. Bake at 450° for 40 to 45 minutes or until browned. Serve immediately with ketchup, if desired.

Chili-Corn Chip
Stack-Up Salad,
page 241

rethinking
leftovers

chili tortilla pie

makes 8 servings · hands-on time 10 min. · total time 47 min.

 **souper tip**

You can use whatever type of bell pepper and onion you prefer to prepare this pie.

With leftover Quick Turkey Chili, this Chili Tortilla Pie will be a cinch to make. Your family will love the layers of flavor and the melted cheese and spices.

Vegetable cooking spray
1   poblano pepper, seeded and thinly sliced
1   medium-size red bell pepper, thinly sliced
1   medium onion, vertically thinly sliced (2 cups)
1   tsp. ground cumin
½   tsp. table salt
¼   tsp. freshly ground black pepper
1   Tbsp. vegetable oil
4½ cups leftover Quick Turkey Chili (page 118), lightly drained
9   (6-inch) corn tortillas, cut in half
1   (8-oz.) package shredded Mexican four-cheese blend
1   (8-oz.) container sour cream
⅓   cup chopped fresh cilantro
¼   cup chopped green onions

1. Preheat oven to 375°. Spray a 3-qt. round ceramic baking dish with cooking spray. Sauté peppers, onion, cumin, salt, and black pepper in hot oil in a large nonstick skillet over medium-high heat, stirring often, 8 minutes or until lightly browned.

2. To assemble dish, spoon 1⅓ cups chili into baking dish. Top with 1 cup vegetable mixture. Top vegetables with 6 corn tortilla halves, slightly overlapping tortillas. Top tortillas with ⅔ cup shredded cheese. Repeat layers 2 times, ending with cheese on top.

3. Bake at 375° for 25 to 30 minutes or until bubbly and cheese is lightly browned. Let stand 5 minutes. Top with sour cream; sprinkle with chopped cilantro and green onions.

portable chili-corn chip pies

makes 6 servings · hands-on time: 5 min. · total time: 5 min.

souper tip

These chili-corn chip pies can be customized to your liking. Feel free to serve them with an assortment of toppings, including corn, chopped bell pepper, sliced fresh jalapeños (or other hot chiles), sliced green onions, and any cheese you like.

You can use whatever leftover chili you prefer in these easy chili pies.

6   (1¼ -oz.) bags corn chips
3   cups warm Playoff Chili (page 103)

Toppings: chopped onion, shredded Cheddar cheese, sour cream

1. Cut corn chip bags open at one long side. Spoon ½ cup chili on chips in each bag. Top with desired amount of onion, Cheddar cheese, and sour cream.

Note: We tested with Fritos Brand Original Corn Chips.

smart solutions for leftover chili

Chili is a tasty meal on its own, but here are some options when you want to think outside the bowl.

Chili Baked Potato:

Bake a russet or sweet potato. Cut potatoes in half lengthwise, and fluff with a fork. Top with warm chili, shredded cheese, and a dollop of sour cream.

Huevos Rancheros:

Heat corn tortillas and chili; keep warm. Scramble eggs. Place a tortilla on each plate, top with eggs and chili. Add shredded cheese, salsa, and sour cream.

Chili-Stuffed Bell Peppers:

Add cooked rice and shredded cheese to leftover chili. Spoon chili mixture into hollowed out bell peppers. Place upright in a 13- x 9-inch baking dish. Bake, covered, at 375° for 30 to 40 minutes.

Chili Dogs:

Grill hot dogs, and place in buns. Spoon warm chili over hot dogs, and top with cheese and chopped onions.

Cornbread Chili Stacks:

Cut baked cornbread into squares; slice horizontally. Top bottom half with warm chili and cheese. Top with remaining half, cut side down, and top with more chili and cheese.

Cincinnati-Style Chili Spaghetti:

Toss warm chili with hot cooked spaghetti. Serve with garlic bread.

Chili Empanadas:

Add a few teaspoons of chili to one side of refrigerated pizza crust dough squares. Fold diagonally to form a triangle, and crimp edges to seal. Bake at 425° for 15 to 17 minutes.

Chili Grits:

Serve warm chili over cheese grits.

Chili Queso Dip:

Add chili to cubed processed cheese, and microwave according to package directions. Stir in salsa, if desired, and serve with tortilla chips.

Chili Pizza:

Spread chili over a prebaked Italian pizza crust, top with shredded Cheddar and mozzarella cheeses. Bake as directed. Top with shredded lettuce and diced tomatoes, and serve.

Chili Cheese Fries:

Bake or fry French fries. Arrange on a platter or individual plates. Top with chili, and sprinkle with shredded cheese.

beef stew shepherd's pie

makes 6 servings · hands-on time 8 min. · total time 28 min.

Refrigerated mashed potatoes make quick work of this weeknight main dish, which also uses leftover beef stew.

3 **cups Red Wine Beef Stew (page 136)**
1 **cup frozen peas, thawed**
1 **(24-oz.) package refrigerated mashed potatoes**

1½ **cups (6 oz.) shredded white Cheddar cheese**
½ **cup chopped green onions**
½ **cup (2 oz.) shredded Cheddar cheese**

1. Preheat oven to 400°.

2. Bring stew to a boil in a large saucepan over medium-high heat; reduce heat, and simmer 4 minutes or until liquid is hot and bubbly. Stir in peas. Spoon into a lightly greased 8-inch-square baking dish.

3. Heat potatoes according to package directions; stir in white Cheddar cheese and green onions. Spoon over stew in baking dish; sprinkle with shredded Cheddar cheese.

4. Bake at 400° for 15 minutes or until cheese melts. Let stand 5 minutes before serving.

spicy pork quesadillas

makes 6 servings · hands-on time 11 min. · total time 28 min.

Using the tender, slow-cooked pork from leftover Mexican Pork Stew makes these quesadillas an easy weeknight dinner with extraordinary flavor.

1	Tbsp. vegetable oil	6	(8-inch) flour tortillas
1	cup thinly sliced onion	1½	cups coarsely chopped radishes
2	garlic cloves, minced		
¼	tsp. chipotle chili powder	½	cup chopped green onions
¼	tsp. table salt	½	cup chopped fresh cilantro
¼	tsp. ground cumin	2	Tbsp. fresh lime juice
4	cups Mexican Pork Stew, drained (page 140)	2	Tbsp. olive oil
		½	tsp. table salt
3	cups (12 oz.) shredded Mexican four-cheese blend		Sour cream (optional)

1. Preheat oven to 200°. Heat oil in a large nonstick skillet over medium-high heat. Add onions; sauté 4 minutes, stirring often, until softened. Add garlic, chili powder, salt, and cumin; sauté 3 minutes. Add drained pork stew, and sauté until ingredients are slightly dry and golden brown. Set aside.

2. Spread ½ cup cheese and ½ cup pork mixture on one side of each tortilla, folding tortilla over to make a half moon. Heat a lightly greased large nonstick skillet over medium-high heat just until hot. Cook quesadillas, in batches, 2 to 3 minutes on each side or until cheese melts and outside is golden brown. Keep quesadillas warm in preheated oven on baking sheet lined with aluminum foil.

3. Combine radishes and next 5 ingredients in a small bowl, tossing well. Serve quesadillas cut into wedges with radish mixture and sour cream, if desired.

basil-pesto pizza

makes 4 servings · hands-on time 8 min. · total time 22 min.

souper tip

If you like your pizza crust a little thicker, use a regular one in place of the thin crust variety called for here. You'll just need to bake the pizza a bit longer to get the crust to a golden brown.

To speed up prep time even more, you can use a prebaked crust.

1   (11-oz.) can refrigerated thin pizza crust dough
⅓   cup Basil Pesto (page 83)
⅓   cup grated Parmesan cheese
8   oz. fresh mozzarella, sliced

3   small plum tomatoes, sliced
1   cup frozen roasted corn, thawed
⅓   cup firmly packed whole basil leaves

1. Preheat oven to 450°. Unroll dough; pat to an even thickness on a lightly greased baking sheet. Bake 7 to 9 minutes or until lightly browned.

2. Spread ⅓ cup Basil Pesto onto crust. Top pizza with Parmesan, mozzarella slices, tomato slices, and corn.

3. Bake at 450° for 6 minutes or until cheese is melted and golden. Remove from oven, and top with basil leaves.

* We tested with Whole Foods frozen roasted corn kernels.

chili-corn chip stack-up salad

makes 4 to 6 servings · hands-on time 15 min. · total time 30 min.

1   (3.5-oz.) package boil-in-bag rice

1   Tbsp. chopped fresh cilantro (optional)

1   (15-oz.) bag corn chips

5   to 6 cups Big-Batch Chili, thawed (page 93)

½   head iceberg lettuce, shredded, or 1 (10-oz.) package shredded iceberg lettuce

1   (8-oz.) package shredded Cheddar-Jack cheese

3   plum tomatoes, chopped

4   green onions, chopped

Sour cream

1   (2.25-oz.) can sliced ripe black olives, drained (optional)

1   (12-oz.) jar pickled jalapeño peppers (optional)

1. Prepare rice according to package directions. Stir in cilantro, if desired.

2. Layer rice mixture, chips, chili, next 5 ingredients, and if desired, black olives and jalapeño peppers in individual serving bowls.

souper tip

To serve, arrange salad ingredients on the kitchen counter or sideboard in the order listed. Have each person spoon rice on a plate first to anchor the stack up and prevent sliding. Add items your family likes, such as corn, chopped bell pepper, and sliced fresh jalapeño peppers.

southwestern taco salad

makes 4 servings · hands-on time 10 min. · total time 10 min.

This Southwestern-inspired taco salad makes good use of leftover Smoky Chicken Chili and is complemented by a chipotle-lime sour cream dressing.

1   cup sour cream
2   Tbsp. fresh lime juice
1½ Tbsp. minced canned chipotle pepper in adobo sauce
⅜   tsp. table salt
2   romaine hearts, chopped
4½ cups Smoky Chicken Chili, drained (page 106)
1   cup frozen fire-roasted corn, thawed*

1   cup (4 oz.) shredded pepper Jack cheese
¼   cup chopped red onion
4   cups restaurant-style tortilla chips*
¼   cup pickled jalapeño pepper slices, drained
3   Tbsp. chopped fresh cilantro

1. Whisk together sour cream and next 3 ingredients.

2. Layer lettuce and remaining ingredients on a serving platter or plates for individual servings. Serve with dressing.

* We tested with Whole Foods frozen fire-roasted corn and Xochitl tortilla chips.

diablo bloody mary

makes 4 servings · hands-on time 15 min. · total time 45 min.

With a quick whir of the blender, Chilled Mexican-Style Salsa Soup is transformed into a spicy Bloody Mary with all the fixin's.

3 cups Chilled Mexican-Style Salsa Soup (page 186)
1 cup vegetable juice*
⅔ cup vodka
1 Tbsp. prepared horseradish
1 tsp. hot sauce*
½ tsp. Worcestershire sauce
1½ Tbsp. fresh lime juice
¼ tsp. freshly ground black pepper
⅛ tsp. table salt
Garnishes: celery sticks, pickled okra, pickled whole jalapeño peppers, large pimiento-stuffed Spanish olives, lime wedges

1. Process soup in a blender until smooth, stopping to scrape down sides as needed. Strain and discard solids.

2. Stir together pureed soup, vegetable juice, vodka, and next 6 ingredients in a pitcher. Refrigerate mixture at least 30 minutes. Serve over ice.

* We tested with V8 and Tabasco red pepper sauce.

mexican layer dip

makes 6 cups · hands-on time 5 min · total time 35 min.

··

Instead of baking this dip, you can also assemble it and serve it chilled.

4   cups leftover Taco Soup, drained (page 48)
Vegetable cooking spray
1   cup salsa verde
⅔   cup frozen roasted corn, thawed*
¼   cup chopped green onions
1   (2¼-oz.) can sliced black olives
1   cup (4 oz.) shredded Mexican four-cheese blend
1   Tbsp. taco seasoning mix
1   (8-oz.) container sour cream
2   Tbsp. chopped fresh cilantro
Tortilla chips

1. Preheat oven to 350°. Spread soup mixture evenly into an 11- x 7-inch baking dish coated with cooking spray. Spread salsa evenly over soup mixture. Combine corn, onions, and olives; spoon corn mixture evenly over salsa. Sprinkle cheese over corn mixture.

2. Bake at 350° for 25 minutes or until bubbly. Let stand 5 minutes. Meanwhile, combine taco seasoning mix and sour cream. Spread over baked dip; sprinkle with cilantro. Serve with tortilla chips.

* We tested with Whole Foods frozen roasted corn kernels.

strawberry-buttermilk ice cream

makes 5½ cups · hands-on time 12 min. · total time 4 hours, 32 min., plus overnight

Adding strawberry preserves near the end of churning, rather than stirring them in, incorporates the preserves evenly throughout the ice cream.

1   cup buttermilk
1   cup heavy cream
½   cup sugar
6   egg yolks

2   cups Chilled Strawberry Soup (page 168)
½   cup strawberry preserves

1. Whisk together first 4 ingredients in a large, heavy saucepan. Cook over medium heat, whisking constantly, 8 to 10 minutes or until mixture thickens slightly. Remove from heat; whisk in Chilled Strawberry Soup until combined. Cool completely (about 1 hour), stirring occasionally. Place heavy-duty plastic wrap directly on warm custard (to prevent a film from forming); chill 8 to 24 hours.

2. Pour mixture into the freezer container of a 1½-qt. electric ice-cream maker, and freeze according to manufacturer's instructions. (Instructions and times may vary.) When ice cream is almost finished churning, gradually pour in preserves. Churn until ice cream is done. Freeze in an airtight container at least 4 hours before serving.

metric equivalents

The recipes that appear in this cookbook use the standard U.S. method for measuring liquid and dry or solid ingredients (teaspoons, tablespoons, and cups). The information on this chart is provided to help cooks outside the United States successfully use these recipes. All equivalents are approximate.

Metric Equivalents for Different Types of Ingredients

A standard cup measure of a dry or solid ingredient will vary in weight depending on the type of ingredient. A standard cup of liquid is the same volume for any type of liquid. Use the following chart when converting standard cup measures to grams (weight) or milliliters (volume).

Standard Cup	Fine Powder (ex. flour)	Grain (ex. rice)	Granular (ex. sugar)	Liquid Solids (ex. butter)	Liquid (ex. milk)
1	140 g	150 g	190 g	200 g	240 ml
¾	105 g	113 g	143 g	150 g	180 ml
⅔	93 g	100 g	125 g	133 g	160 ml
½	70 g	75 g	95 g	100 g	120 ml
⅓	47 g	50 g	63 g	67 g	80 ml
¼	35 g	38 g	48 g	50 g	60 ml
⅛	18 g	19 g	24 g	25 g	30 ml

Useful Equivalents for Dry Ingredients by Weight

(To convert ounces to grams, multiply the number of ounces by 30.)

1 oz	=	1/16 lb	=	30 g
4 oz	=	¼ lb	=	120 g
8 oz	=	½ lb	=	240 g
12 oz	=	¾ lb	=	360 g
16 oz	=	1 lb	=	480 g

Useful Equivalents for Length

(To convert inches to centimeters, multiply the number of inches by 2.5.)

1 in			=	2.5 cm		
6 in	=	½ ft	=	15 cm		
12 in	=	1 ft	=	30 cm		
36 in	=	3 ft	=	1 yd	=	90 cm
40 in			=	100 cm	=	1 m

Useful Equivalents for Liquid Ingredients by Volume

¼ tsp					=	1 ml	
½ tsp					=	2 ml	
1 tsp					=	5 ml	
3 tsp	=	1 Tbsp		=	½ fl oz	=	15 ml
		2 Tbsp	=	⅛ cup	=	1 fl oz	=	30 ml
		4 Tbsp	=	¼ cup	=	2 fl oz	=	60 ml
		5⅓ Tbsp	=	⅓ cup	=	3 fl oz	=	80 ml
		8 Tbsp	=	½ cup	=	4 fl oz	=	120 ml
		10⅔ Tbsp	=	⅔ cup	=	5 fl oz	=	160 ml
		12 Tbsp	=	¾ cup	=	6 fl oz	=	180 ml
		16 Tbsp	=	1 cup	=	8 fl oz	=	240 ml
		1 pt	=	2 cups	=	16 fl oz	=	480 ml
		1 qt	=	4 cups	=	32 fl oz	=	960 ml
					33 fl oz	=	1000 ml	= 1 l

Useful Equivalents for Cooking/Oven Temperatures

	Fahrenheit	Celsius	Gas Mark
Freeze water	32° F	0° C	
Room temperature	68° F	20° C	
Boil water	212° F	100° C	
Bake	325° F	160° C	3
	350° F	180° C	4
	375° F	190° C	5
	400° F	200° C	6
	425° F	220° C	7
	450° F	230° C	8
Broil			Grill

index

Previously published as
Southern Living® Soups, Stews & Chilis
©2014 by Time Home Entertainment Inc.

ISBN-13: 9-780-8487-4705-3
ISBN-10: 0-8487-4705-4
Library of Congress Control Number: 2015944229
Printed in the United States of America
First Printing 2015

Editor: Rachel Quinlivan West, R.D.
Editorial Assistant: April Smitherman
Project Editor: Emily Chappell Connolly
Assistant Designer: Allison Sperando Potter
Assistant Test Kitchen Manager:
    Alyson Moreland Haynes
Photographer: Johnny Autry
Senior Photo Stylists: Kay E. Clarke,
    Mindi Shapiro Levine
Food & Photo Stylist: Charlotte Autry
Senior Production Managers: Greg Amason,
    Sue Chodakiewicz
Copy Editors: Jacqueline Giovanelli, Barry Smith
Proofreader: Rebecca Henderson
Indexer: Nanette Cardon
Fellows: Kylie Dazzo, Elizabeth Laseter

COVER: Veggie Chili (page 122), Loaded Potato Soup (page 71), Mexican Pork Stew (page 140), Pork Dumpling Soup (page 51)